CHESHIRE
MURDER CASEBOOK

STEVE FIELDING

COUNTRYSIDE BOOKS
NEWBURY · BERKSHIRE

CONTENTS

INTRODUCTION

It was in London in the middle of the 18th century that Henry Fielding created the Bow Street Runners, the first attempt at an organised body of men specifically collected together to help fight a sharp increase in crime. Some 50 or so years later, this ideal was taken a step further when Sir Robert Peel set up what we recognise now as the first police force: the Metropolitan Police Force was created in 1829.

In that same year, Cheshire became the first county to follow Sir Robert Peel's lead, appointing nine Stipendiary Deputy High Constables to supervise a scratch force of petty constables. In 1835, Parliament passed the Municipal Corporation Act which empowered boroughs with a population over a certain size to establish their own local police force, and among the first to do so were Chester and Warrington.

As the region became more industrialised, the population of the county increased dramatically. In 1801 the population of Cheshire was 191,000, and this rose to more than double, 420,000, just 50 years later. Immigrant workers from Ireland, Scotland and many from across the Welsh borders flocked to the area to work in the coal and salt mines, on the farms and in the new chemical industry – the country's first chemical works had opened at Widnes in 1847. With the advent of the railways, workers also settled in Crewe, which soon became one of the biggest railway towns in England.

The increase in population also brought with it an increase in crime and to combat this, a radical revision of the policing system took place. The borough police forces were soon superseded by a county force and in 1857 Captain Thomas Smith became the first Chief Constable of the new Cheshire Constabulary.

The Cheshire Constabulary, like its contemporaries across the country, took advantage of the great strides made in both crime

5

detection and forensic science. Fingerprinting and blood-grouping, along with radio technology and the motor car, all went some way towards helping the police become more efficient. These were followed by the creation of the CID, the acceptance of women police officers, and the formation of the fire brigade, which took away another task from the already overworked bobby.

Punishment for offenders in the 18th and 19th centuries was swift and severe. Many crimes which today would carry a light prison sentence carried the death penalty, and a trawl through early records shows that in October 1786 a man named John Hyde was hanged at Boughton for horse theft. A month later, James Buckley was hanged on the same gallows for burglary. In August 1861, Martin Doyle became the last man hanged in Great Britain for any offence other than murder or treachery/treason, when he was hanged at Chester Gaol for attempted murder.

In the early days murderers committing their crimes in Cheshire were hanged at Chester. In the 18th century executions took place in public at Boughton, and by 1801 they were being held on Northgate. Later public executions took place at both the House of Correction and the Castle Gaol. The last execution at Chester took place in 1883, when Patrick Carey was hanged for a murder near Congleton. The story of Carey's dreadful crime is recalled in Chapter 2 of this casebook.

In 1886, the trapdoors crashed open for the first time at Knutsford Gaol, when the first of eight felons to end their lives on the gallows there was hanged. The eight were:

1. 22nd February 1886 – Owen McGill (39): an Irish-born farm labourer who beat his wife to death at Birkenhead.

2. 16th August 1887 – Thomas Henry Bevan (20): an apprentice iron-moulder from Crewe who battered his aunt to death.

3. 8th April 1890 – Richard Davies (18): convicted along with his 16 year old brother George of the murder of their bullying father on a road outside Crewe. Both were sentenced to death but shortly before the executions were scheduled, George was reprieved on account of his age. The hangman, James Berry, recalled later that the face of Richard Davies repeatedly came back to haunt him.

4. 22nd August 1890 – Felix Spicer (60): murdered two of his children and attempted to murder his wife, by cutting their throats, at New Brighton.

5. 9th August 1905 – William Hancocks (35): stabbed his daughter to death at Birkenhead.

6. 27th November 1906 – Edward Hartigan (58): battered his wife to death at Stockport.

7. 12th November 1908 – James Phipps (21): sexually assaulted and murdered a young girl at Winsford.

8. 19th March 1912 – John Williams (38): murdered his wife by cutting her throat at Birkenhead.

In 1863, one of the most infamous murders in Victorian Cheshire took place. Alice Holt was convicted and later executed for the murder, by poisoning, of her mother. This controversial case was recently the subject of a television programme which questioned the guilt of the accused.

Unsurprisingly, by virtue of its size and population, Cheshire cannot claim to have had a large share of infamous murders. That said, though, the murder at Gorse Hall in 1909 made the headlines across the country, as did the horrific murder of three French tourists in 1971. Both these cases are fully recorded in the following chapters.

I hope that the pages of this and similar murder casebooks are the closest the reader will come to murder. With the clear-up rate by the Cheshire Constabulary one of the highest in the country, residents of the county can feel safe in the knowledge that their police are among the most diligent in the land.

Steve Fielding
Autumn 1996

1
AN
INSIDE JOB

The Murder of Patrick Tracey at Widnes
October 1879

From the outset the police had their suspicions. They were investigating the murder of Patrick Tracey, a 36 year old Irish-born father of three, who, in the early hours of Friday 24th October 1879, had been shot dead in his bed at his home in Oxford Street, Newton, Widnes; as the first statements were taken, several facts just didn't ring true.

It was the victim's wife, 28 year old Mary-Anne Tracey, who had raised the alarm, and she told the police that sometime between 1 and 2 am she had been startled by the sound of gunshots. Shocked into waking suddenly, Mrs Tracey said she was so stunned and frightened by the terrible noise that she couldn't see anything, but as she finally came round, she noticed that there was a strong smell of smoke and powder in the room.

'I tried to raise my husband,' she told the officer, 'but he was bleeding from wounds to the head.' She said that she hurried down the landing to rouse their two Irish lodgers, Hugh Burns and Patrick Kearns. Both men were sent out: Burns was told to fetch the family doctor, Dr O'Keefe, while Kearns was dispatched to find Father Clarke. By the time the doctor and the priest had arrived at the house, Patrick Tracey was dead.

The police were duly called and under the watchful eye of senior officers, Dr O'Keefe examined the body of Patrick Tracey. He found a large gash on the side of the victim's head and from inside he removed a large bullet which had pierced the brain. 'In my opinion,' the doctor told the police, 'death would have been instantaneous.'

The likely murder weapon was soon recovered when an officer

9

spotted a pistol lying in an adjacent alley. Upon close examination it was found to fire bullets of the same calibre as the one removed from the victim's head.

Although Patrick Tracey worked as a labourer at 'Messrs Platt's', a local chemical works, he had amassed savings of some £20, money which he had sewn into a cloth, which in turn was wrapped in a bag and hidden in a locked strongbox kept in the kitchen. This strongbox had been prised open, apparently by a chisel, and the contents were missing.

Initially it was thought that the murder was the work of a man who had already killed before. Police at Widnes were still investigating the murder of Patrick Delaney who been found dead in suspicious circumstances a few months earlier, but as statements were made at the scene of the crime, the more experienced officers began to suspect an 'inside job'.

The first seeds of suspicion were sewn when the victim's wife made her statement. She told police that the killer would probably have gained entry by climbing through the rear kitchen window which she had inadvertently left open. This couldn't have been the case, as keen-eyed officers noticed cobwebs across the frame which would have been disturbed if this had happened.

A neighbour told police that shortly before the shots were fired, she had heard the sound of heavy footsteps on the landing, and suspicion was intensified when Mrs Tracey was asked to show police the nightgown she had been wearing at the time of her husband's murder. Instead of finding traces of the blood which had spattered from the wound and had covered the wall above the bed and the bedding, police discovered that Mrs Tracey's nightdress was suspiciously free of any sign of blood. This seemed to indicate that she could not have been lying beside her husband when he was shot. If she wasn't sleeping by his side in the early hours, then where could she have been? With one of the lodgers, perhaps?

Detectives also found it hard to imagine that neither lodger would have heard the gunshots, although both gave statements to this effect, saying that they had had to be roused by Mrs Tracey banging on the bedroom door shouting that her husband had been murdered. It had been Burns who had answered the door and who had followed Mrs Tracey downstairs to fetch a light. Both men were out of work, and despite the fact that evidence suggested that Mrs Tracey was not telling police the truth, it was the two men who were arrested on suspicion and taken into custody.

Evidence against the two men grew apace. At an inquest held a fortnight after the murder, a pawnbroker's assistant told police that he had sold a pistol similar to the murder weapon a week or so before the murder, whilst Mr Jervis, the ironmonger on Victoria Road, Widnes, identified Hugh Burns as a man who had purchased some powder, shot and caps at the shop three days before the murder. He also identified Kearns as the man who had waited outside the shop during the sale.

Medical experts confirmed that no one could have been lying next to the victim when he was shot and not be covered in blood, and this put Mrs Tracey back in the frame. Further proof that she was implicated in the murder was shown when it was revealed that she had three insurance policies, at different offices, for a combined total of £365.

At the inquest the jury, after deliberating for one hour, returned to find guilty verdicts against both lodgers and, to the surprise of many in the court, they also found Mrs Tracey guilty. This was something of a shock as Mrs Tracey had merely attended the inquest as a witness and up until that moment had not been charged with any offence.

Clearly taken aback, the coroner said that his job was merely to record the verdict, even if, as in this case, he disagreed with the findings. After conferring with the foreman of the jury, he told the packed court that the inquest jury believed that Mrs Tracey was implicated in the murder and if she was innocent she would have ample chance to clear her name at the court hearing.

The trial of Hugh Burns, Patrick Kearns and Mary-Anne Tracey for what was dubbed 'a crime of singular and atrocious character' opened at Liverpool Assizes on Thursday 12th February 1880, before Baron Coleridge.

In the intervening time between inquest and trial, several things had occurred, the most notable being that Kearns had made a statement while being held at Kirkdale Prison. Kearns, who was 21, had told officers that 30 year old Burns was the killer, even going on to describe his version of the events of that night.

A further statement was supplied by a friend of Mrs Tracey, who said that since the murder the widow lived in fear of Burns and Big Paddy (Kearns) coming to shoot her and the children. One other thing no one in the packed courtroom could have failed to notice as Mrs Tracey took her place in the dock was that she was heavily pregnant.

As the trial began, Mr Heywood, for the prosecution, outlined the facts. 'There is no doubt that Patrick Tracey was murdered in his bed,' he began, 'the question is whether he was murdered by the other inmates of the house, or by someone who had broken into the house for the purpose of robbery.' Most of the evidence from the inquest was reheard in the court and when it came to the question of the various insurance policies, the prosecution told of a fourth and hitherto unknown document which had only recently come to light in which Mrs Tracey had taken out another policy for £100.

The prosecution also told the court that despite claiming there was money in the kitchen, it was a fact that Mrs Tracey was running into debt. The final point made by the Crown was to claim that no one could have gained entry into the house on the night of the murder, unless admitted by someone inside.

Countering the point on the insurance policies, the defence counsel claimed that it was not such an unusual occurrence for a wife to take out a policy for her husband, especially as he was the father of three young children and was employed in such a dangerous working environment.

At the conclusion of their evidence, defence counsel addressed the jury. They pointed out that besides proving a motive and ability to commit a crime, it must be also proven that no other person had committed it, and in this case this had not been done. Finishing his summing up, the judge said that if the jury believed that any of the accused had carried out the crime alone, then he or she alone would be guilty, but if they believed that all three had acted in consort, then each was equally guilty. After just 20 minutes the jury returned to find all the accused guilty of murder. With a black cap draped upon his wig, Baron Coleridge sentenced all three to death.

It was clear that Mrs Tracey, because of her condition, would not be hanged, and official word came through on the next day that her sentence was commuted to one of life imprisonment.

Within a week of being sentenced, Kearns made another dramatic statement. Now he claimed that Burns was innocent of any crime and that it was he who had committed the murder in league with Mary-Anne Tracey; while he admitted to knowing who had fired the gun that night, he wouldn't name names, other than saying that he and Mrs Tracey were having an affair and had planned the crime together. He made a further statement that he was prepared to face the consequences for the murder but that the sentence of Burns was unjust, and he asked for the Home Secretary to intervene.

As the days ebbed away to the execution date, scheduled for 2nd March, no word was heard from London regarding the fate of Burns. Strenuous efforts were made to obtain his release on the basis of Kearns's confession and on the ground that even during the trial the best evidence that the prosecution could come up with in regard to Burns was that he *may* have been promised a share of the insurance money. Burns himself had protested all along that he was innocent, and although he had purchased the powder and shot from the iron-monger's, this was at the instruction of Kearns.

It was suggested by his counsel that after the trial, Burns, who lived in fear of Kearns and was not the most articulate of men, having seen the mesh woven around him, had fallen into sullen despair and unaccountable apathy. Prompted by an inability to refute many of the certainly telling circumstances, he calmly resigned himself to whatever fate awaited him. When Kearns's statement was made known, however, he began to assert his innocence in the strongest terms.

Remarkably, in the face of the evidence, Burns, protesting his innocence to the last, took his place beside Kearns on the gallows on the appointed morning. The sordid, unhappy case took a further twist when it was later announced that Kearns was the father of the child Mrs Tracey gave birth to, behind the prison walls.

Was an innocent man hanged? On the evidence available it seems that a very real miscarriage of justice may have taken place that snow-covered morning at Kirkdale Prison, Liverpool, when executioner William Marwood, with his usual ruthless efficiency, dispatched Burns and Kearns to the next world.

2
MURDER
AT THE INN

The Murders of Thomas Earlam and Mary
Mohan at Smallwood
February 1883

Sixty-four year old Thomas Earlam was a former farmer and potato dealer who had given up the family business to run a lowly hostelry at Smallwood, a tiny hamlet standing on the main road linking Congleton and Sandbach.

The guesthouse was spartan and very basic, with the bulk of the trade comprised of farm labourers, travellers and itinerant tramps. Although Earlam was not a wealthy man, the house did a reasonable trade, helped no doubt by its position on the main route linking Manchester and the Potteries. Sharing the house with Thomas Earlam was Mary Mohan, his live-in housekeeper who was also in her mid-sixties, and a number of local farm labourers who had been resident for many weeks.

It was one of the lodgers who discovered the bodies. At 3 pm on 9th February 1883, Edward Sampey returned to the house and saw Earlam and Mary Mohan lying on the kitchen floor. The floor was covered in blood and from the state of the place it was clear that a dreadful act had been perpetrated.

The police were called and they were soon joined at the house by Charles Latham, a surgeon from nearby Sandbach. Latham pronounced Earlam dead but found that Mary was alive though unlikely to survive her injuries; this was indeed the case, but she remained in a coma for a further week. The murder weapon was found to be a heavy hammer covered in blood and lying on the carpet in the adjacent room.

It was suspected that robbery was the motive for the fearful crime. Earlam's trouser pockets had been turned out and a number of drawers had been ransacked. A list of suspects was drawn up and at the top was a 37 year old tramp by the name of Patrick Carey. Carey, also known as John White, had been a lodger at the house for several days, up until that morning, and from the testimonies of several people it appeared that he had been the last person seen in the house.

Earlier that afternoon he had been seen walking away from the house carrying a bundle of clothes. A suit of clothes belonging to another of the lodgers was missing, and also a few sovereigns known to be in the safe, which was lying open.

As more and more statements were gathered it became clear that Carey would have to be brought in for questioning, if only to clear his name. A detailed description of him was issued in the national press but efforts to trace his whereabouts proved difficult and for a number of weeks police throughout the region pulled out all the stops to find him.

Police in Manchester were asked to work on the case and their inquiries led them to a run-down boarding house in a suburb of the city. Detective Sergeant Jackson and Detective Fox questioned a man at a slum house on Charter Street owned by a Mary Murphy. He gave his name as John Delaney and an address in Elkington, Derbyshire. The officers were not convinced that he was telling the truth and he was asked to accompany them to the city centre police station. 'Mr Delaney' was asked to wait in the corridor, where he was identified as Carey by a lodger who had shared a room with him at Smallwood, and who had been brought to Manchester to help with inquiries.

Under questioning, Delaney admitted that his name was Patrick Carey and whilst he then admitted being a former lodger, he pleaded ignorance of the reported murder. Carey was held in custody whilst evidence was amassed to prove his guilt. When police were satisfied that he was the killer, he was arraigned to stand trial before Mr Justice Hawkins at Chester Assizes on 17th April 1883.

The trial opened with the prosecution counsel, Mr Marshall, outlining the Crown's case. Carey, he said, was, by his own admission the last person in the house on the morning of the murder. A witness who knew him well saw him walking away from the house. The clothes missing from the guesthouse were found in Carey's possession after his arrest.

Ernest Gordon told the court that he was passing the house at 12.15 pm that day and saw Carey and the old man in the house together. He said he was walking along the road and saw them clearly through the window.

A Manchester publican told the court how he had seen Carey in the company of Mary Murphy in the bar of the Crown and Shuttle Inn, Long Millgate, holding a bundle of clothes.

Two shopkeepers came forward to say that Carey had purchased clothes from them and in each case he had tendered a sovereign as payment. A witness also took the stand to say that she had purchased a greatcoat from Carey identified as the one he was wearing when seen shortly after the murders.

The final evidence was given by two medical experts. Charles Latham, the surgeon who had been called to the murder scene, told the court that Earlam had suffered horrendous injuries. The right side of his head had been completely smashed. The temporal bone had been broken up so severely that small fragments of bone were lodged in the brain. The cheek and jawbone were likewise shattered. The surgeon told the packed courtroom that the first blow to the temple would have been enough to cause the victim's death. Fortunately, death would have been mercifully quick.

Mary Mohan had similar injuries to the left side of her face. The beating had not been as severe, although her cheek and jawbone were both broken. Dr Latham said that when he examined her, the whole of the left side of her face was one large purple bruise. She had never regained consciousness and died from her injuries a short time later.

Joseph Carter Bell, the Chester City Analyst, testified that he had found traces of blood on a pair of trousers that Carey was alleged to have been wearing on the day in question, but under cross-examination he had to admit that, other than being sure it was human blood, he couldn't say for certain that it was the same type as that of either victim.

Although the case against the prisoner seemed strong, the defence counsel, Mr Colt Williams, called upon the jury to consider that the evidence in the case was purely circumstantial and not sufficiently strong for them to find Carey guilty of murder. No defence witnesses were called and as the law stood at the time, Carey was not allowed to speak for himself from the dock.

Williams made a spirited effort on his client's behalf. He picked at the statements made by the various witnesses who had allegedly seen Carey walking away from the guesthouse, and in particular he got the witness Gordon to admit that he couldn't be absolutely certain that the man he had seen with Earlam through the window was the prisoner in the dock.

Chester Castle. Patrick Carey was the last person to be hanged here, on 8th May 1883.

Referring to the statement made by the City Analyst, he said that only one spot of blood had been found on the trousers, and it was unlikely that there would be so little spoiling given the terrible state of the kitchen, which the police had earlier described as having blood spattered along the walls and heavy soaking on the floor.

'Surely, the killer would have been heavily bloodstained,' he told the court, reminding them that no one who saw Carey on the road that day had mentioned that he was covered in blood.

Of course, Carey had sported a greatcoat as he walked away, one he later sold in Manchester, and the long coat would effectively disguise any stains if it was put on after the murders had been committed. This point was quickly picked up by the prosecution.

After Williams had concluded the defence's case the judge summed up the salient points, telling the jury that they must be totally satisfied as to the prisoner's guilt if they were to find him guilty of wilful murder. The all-male jury needed a deliberation of just six minutes before returning to find the prisoner guilty as charged.

Donning a black cap, Mr Justice Hawkins, in sombre voice, passed sentence of death:

'Patrick Carey, upon the clearest and most conclusive evidence you have been found guilty of the crime of wilful murder, and no man who has listened attentively to the evidence as it has been offered before the jury can entertain any shadow of a doubt that notwithstanding your observation to the contrary, you are guilty of the wicked and cruel crime of which the jury have just convicted you.

'The law of this country commands me to pass upon you the sentence of death, and your crime is of so cruel, so brutal, and so barbarous a character that when you leave the dock to descend to the prison from whence you came, reflect and feel that your days are numbered, and I can only beseech you during the few hours that are left to you of life to endeavour to seek from that almighty and all-merciful God whose commandment, "Thou shall do no murder", you have so wickedly broken . . .'

Sentence of death was then passed in the accustomed fashion and Carey was removed from the dock. It was recorded that Carey, sitting below in the cell awaiting transportation back to Chester Castle, wept uncontrollably.

At 8 am on Tuesday 8th May 1883, Patrick Carey, also known as John White, had the dubious honour of being the last person hanged at Chester Castle.

3

THE
GORSE HALL MYSTERY

The Murder of George Storrs at Dukinfield
November 1909

Gorse Hall, a spacious mansion standing in its own extensive grounds, was a fitting residence for a successful and wealthy mill-owner such as George Henry Storrs. Storrs was a self-made man. Under his astute management, the family building firm prospered and by 1900 the business had expanded to include cotton mills, timber, and brick manufacture. He was respected and liked well enough by his employees, but few people really knew him. Despite the wealth at his disposal and his considerable standing and status in the community, he was not given to largesse or levity, preferring to spend his free time at home at Gorse Hall, Dukinfield.

Living with him at Gorse Hall was Margaret, his wife of 18 years, to whom he had been introduced by his former neighbours, John and Annie Lindley. Maggie, as his wife preferred to be called, and Annie were sisters and there was much joy when George and Maggie married on 11th August 1891. A few months later, John and Annie died, so their daughter Marion, aged nine, was adopted by the Storrs. Her presence at Gorse Hall brought some life to the place, which despite its imposing millstone-grit exterior, was a sparse and austere home – both George and Maggie preferred a frugal and reserved existence.

Like all gentlefolk of that era, they kept a small domestic staff, comprising a cook, Mary Evans, housemaid Eliza Cook and coachman James Worrall, who lived on the estate with his wife Sarah. Worrall was not only a servant, but also a friend to George Storrs, and despite the conventions of the day, which would have disapproved of such a friendship, the two men would spend hours talking and walking through the surrounding woodland.

The kitchen at Gorse Hall.

The peace and quiet of Gorse Hall was shattered, however, on the evening of 10th September 1909, when James Worrall ran to Stalybridge police station to raise the alarm that shots had been fired at Gorse Hall. Police rushed up the hill to the Hall, but after examining the dining room, where the window was said to have been shattered by the gunshot, and after speaking to 49 year old George Storrs about the incident, they remained dubious and were privately of the opinion that the sound of smashing glass had been confused with gunshots. It was also debated whether Storrs might have orchestrated the incident, with a view to encouraging the police to keep a more watchful eye on his property.

Whatever the truth, a night-time police guard began at Gorse Hall; an alarm bell was also purchased, which was installed on the roof of the house, and was large enough to be heard downhill at the police station should the need arise.

The need arose some six weeks later, on Friday 29th October 1909, when midnight slumbers were broken by the clanging of the bell. The

Gorse Hall, Dukinfield.

police again rushed up the hill to Gorse Hall, this time to be met by George Storrs in the porch of his home, pocket watch in hand, having engineered this 'drill' to establish the response time of the local bobbies.

The police, remembering their previous inconclusive visit to Gorse Hall, were irritated by this second wasted journey, and unbeknown to George Storrs, the nightwatch was withdrawn from his house on 1st November, and redeployed more effectively on crowd control during the elections at Stalybridge.

At 9.15 pm on 1st November, Mr and Mrs Storrs and Marion Lindley were chatting in the dining room, whilst cook Mary Evans prepared supper. The cook was startled to see a man lurking by the kitchen door and at first mistook him for Worrall, the coachman. She realised it was not him when the man crossed the kitchen and held a revolver to her head. She kept her wits about her and managed to run from the kitchen, trying to close the door behind her. She ran down a hallway, nearly colliding with Eliza Cook, who then found herself confronting the intruder. Eliza was rendered motionless, but Mary Evans ran on to the dining room.

'There's a man in the house,' she screamed, as George and Maggie Storrs ran down the hallway. Storrs grabbed the man's wrist and tried to

21

George Henry Storrs.

loosen his grip on the revolver, while Maggie seized an ornamental cudgel and took aim to strike the intruder. Seeing the raised shillelagh, he told her: 'I will not shoot', and passed the gun to her.

She ran upstairs with it and rang the alarm bell, while Marion Lindley, Eliza Cook and Mary Evans ran to fetch help. Eliza and Mary were dismayed that coachman Worrall was not at home, but as it turned out he was taking a drink locally, heard the alarm bell and raced to the Hall. He met a party of eight men summoned by Marion from the Liberal Club, and they told him of the scene they had found on arrival at Gorse Hall.

George Storrs was lying on the kitchen floor in a pool of blood, but still conscious, and concerned for the welfare of his wife. Henry Heald, one of the party of eight, asked George who had attacked him, but he ignored this question and asked after his wife again. She ran down the stairs to him and he died moments later. He had been stabbed some 15 times, and although the attacker had taken the knife with him, the police took possession of the revolver the intruder had surrendered to Maggie.

The gun, an 'American Bullock', was broken, and had clearly been used to frighten. Vague descriptions of the man, offered by the four women who had each seen him only briefly, were all the police had to go on, and although officers from both Stalybridge and Dukinfield joined the investigation, a lack of specific information led them to make a commendably prompt but contentious arrest.

Thirty-one year old Cornelius Howard was a cousin of the late George Storrs, but there was little similarity between them in lifestyle or temperament. Apart from a period in the army, Howard had spent most of his adult life in and out of prison for burglary. He was arrested at Oldham on 17th November, when true to form, he was attempting to break into a shop.

He had a cast-iron alibi for his movements prior to 7th October, as he was serving a sentence at Wakefield Gaol. Although a thief, he had no record for violence, and there was nothing to associate him with the murder other than the outcome of an identity parade which took place on the day after his arrest.

Mrs Storrs found no resemblance in Howard to the attacker, but both Mary Evans and Eliza Cook thought he 'looked like the man', although neither could be sure – unlike Marion Lindley, who observed the line-up, pointed to Howard and confidently declared: 'That's the man!'

William Leah, Deputy Chief Constable of Cheshire, discussed the

Cornelius Howard.

outcome of the identity parade with senior colleagues and later that day Inspector Brewster charged Howard with the murder of George Storrs.

On Thursday 3rd March 1910, Cornelius Howard faced Mr Justice Pickford and a 12-man jury, from the dock at Chester Assizes. His counsel made short, if polite, work of the four lady witnesses to the crime, countering their identification with the brevity of their contact with the assailant.

The Crown's case was at best weak. Mr Francis Williams, leading for the prosecution, had no forensic or scientific evidence against the accused and Howard's alibi, that he was in Huddersfield on the night of the murder, had been substantiated.

The trial lasted two days and shortly after 6 pm on the Friday, the jury retired to consider its verdict. Twenty minutes later they returned to find Howard not guilty. Cheers rang out from the packed gallery as the verdict was announced.

Whether through genuine zeal to solve the murder, or a wish to restore their reputation after the flimsy case against Howard, the police pressed on. In the meantime, Storrs's widow, legally adopted daughter and staff left the Hall and moved to the Lake District; Gorse Hall was boarded up, awaiting demolition.

On 23rd June 1910, Mark Wilde was arrested on a charge of attempted murder, after slashing out with a knife at a young cotton worker out strolling with his girl near Gorse Hall, three days earlier. Inspector Brewster connected 28 year old Wilde's physical appearance to the description given months earlier of the Gorse Hall murderer, and further questioning established that Wilde had owned two guns.

Wilde, fearful that his guns might connect him in some way to the murder of George Storrs, told the police that one of them had broken and he had discarded it some months ago. But this fact now did link him with the crime, as the gun that the police had in custody was also broken.

Convicted of the assault on the cotton worker, Wilde served two months in Knutsford Gaol. This was an unusually light sentence for such a serious crime, and seems to have been 'arranged' so that evidence linking him to the Gorse Hall murder could be gathered.

A week before the end of his sentence, Wilde took part in an identity parade where he was picked out by Mary Evans and Eliza Cook. Mrs Storrs failed to identify him, while Marion Lindley thought he slightly resembled the attacker. On 30th August 1910, Wilde walked out of

Knutsford Gaol only to be immediately arrested and charged with the murder of George Storrs.

Mr Justice Horridge presided over his trial at Chester on 24th October. If anything, the evidence here was weaker than at the first trial. Called to give evidence for the prosecution, the four ladies again told the court they believed the man in the dock was the man who had murdered George Storrs. Sparing them no embarrassment, defence counsel Mr Edward Nelson KC pointed out that in this same courtroom just six months earlier they had each pointed to another man in the dock with the same accusation. Police evidence linking Wilde to the gun found at the scene of the crime was at best tenuous and was also swiftly dealt with.

Although in this case the trial took five days to reach its conclusion, the result was the same. Again the jury needed less than one hour to acquit the prisoner. Mark Wilde celebrated his acquittal with a party at a Manchester hotel, joined in the celebrations by Cornelius Howard. Wilde was indeed a fortunate man, for in the haste to try him for the Gorse Hall murder he had served just a fraction of the usual sentence for attempted murder.

The identity of the murderer at Gorse Hall remains a mystery. Of the house itself nothing now remains – it was demolished shortly after the acquittal of Cornelius Howard. There was, however, one other incident of note.

George Storrs's coachman and long-time friend James Worrall committed suicide, by hanging himself in a barn at the Hall a week before Howard was arrested. No reason was ever found for the suicide other than grief at his master's death. Did he go to his grave holding a secret, or did a guilty man escape justice when both accused walked from the dock? It is a mystery that remains to this day.

4

THE
UNWANTED SUITOR

The Murder of Frances Johnson at Macclesfield
September 1915

Of all the types of murder committed, crimes of passion are amongst the most common. The tragic case of unrequited love leading to murder that occurred at Macclesfield during the dark days of the First World War is a typical example.

For over two and a half years railwayman John James Thornley had been courting Frances Johnson, a ring spinner in a Macclesfield cotton mill. At 26 years old, and some two years older than his sweetheart, Thornley had yet to be called up for army service and was working as a lampman on the local railway, when in the summer of 1915, their relationship ended.

The break-up was clearly instigated by Frances and stemmed from the fact that both were of different temperaments. She was bright and vivacious while he was sterner and more serious, and as their relationship continued she found that they had little in common and not much prospect of a happy future together.

Thornley initially seemed to pay no heed to Frances's rejection of him, and still regularly turned up at her house, until she finally confided in her father who had a quiet word with the unwanted suitor and warned him off. Although the unwanted visits caused Frances a little distress, she treated them as a nuisance, as there was nothing in his manner to suggest that anything unpleasant would result. When September came around, her parents went ahead with their annual holiday to Cleethorpes. In previous years Frances had accompanied them but this year, because of war work, she was unable to take the time off.

As a result she was left alone at the house, and for company invited her neighbour, May Warren, to stay some nights with her. Knowing that Frances's parents were away on holiday, Thornley took to following the girls around, but they looked on this as a minor inconvenience rather than a serious threat. Indeed, on one instance he called at the house and entered uninvited, but they were able to placate him and he left the house without any untoward incident.

For the first two nights the girls shared Frances's parents' large double bed and spent the early hours chatting away until they fell asleep. Both had to rise for work before dawn, and after two almost sleepless nights they decided that for the rest of May's stay they would sleep in separate rooms to enable them to get a good night's sleep.

On Friday evening, 17th September, Frances and May visited a local theatre where they chanced upon Thornley. The meeting was entirely coincidental, but when he tried to make conversation with them they were brusque with their replies and made it clear they didn't want his attentions. Nevertheless, Thornley followed them into the theatre but took a seat some distance away and made no further contact with them.

Returning home in the early hours, Frances locked all the doors, prepared a fire and breakfast for the morning and set the alarm clock for 4.30 am. What transpired during the night was later recalled by Miss Warren:

'I was awoken at about 2.30 in the morning. I heard a bang in the yard. My first thoughts were that someone was trying to break in, so I listened quietly. Next I heard the rattle of a window as though someone had succeeded in forcing it, and then my alarm increased as I heard footsteps inside the house. My fears were confirmed when I heard someone knock against a table in the darkness. Not a sound up to this time had come from the bedroom in which Frances lay. When I heard the handle on the kitchen door being lifted I tried to muster up my courage to go to warn Frances. Springing out of my bed, I got half-way along the landing when there was a crash, and, glued to the spot for a few seconds with fear, I made out the dark form of a man on the stairs.'

Joseph Barber, May's brother-in-law who lived nearby and happened to be passing that morning, raised the alarm and told the police of his grim discovery. 'I removed a pillow from her [Frances's] face and saw deep wounds like stab wounds, in her throat. Her face was also cut and there was blood on her cheek and arms.'

The police arrived with a Dr Marshall and found a shoemaker's knife at the murder scene. Although placed in Frances's left hand, it was clear from the medical examination that it had been placed there after rigor mortis had set in, effectively ruling out any possibility of suicide. This view was further supported by a letter found on a downstairs table, the contents of which pointed to the involvement of one John James Thornley.

Chief Constable Henry Sheasby organised an immediate search for Thornley, and information from a John Hatton caused them to concentrate their search on an area by the canal near Buxton Road bridge. Hatton, the licensee of the Puss in Boots Inn, had seen a man behaving strangely as he looked out from his bedroom window at 5 am that Saturday morning. The man removed his hat, coat, waistcoat and boots, and swam across the canal and back. Hatton then hastened to the nearby home of Inspector Sproson, who was soon joined on the canal bank by Chief Constable Sheasby and a number of his officers.

Another who had witnessed the strange goings-on was boatman James Hall, who had seen a man on the towpath between Buxton Road and Hurdsfield Road bridges. It was still dark and Hall could not see the man's face clearly, but he said that the man made off in the direction of Hurdsfield.

Later that morning the canal was dragged but nothing unusual was found, so inquiries continued and a description of the wanted man was circulated in the immediate and nearby areas. Details of his build and complexion were given, but the most identifiable feature of Thornley were his numerous tattoos: his upper body was covered in a myriad of colourful designs.

Hunger eventually drove Thornley from his hide-out in the dense woodland at Higher Poynton and on Sunday at 10.30 am, he called at nearby Hagg Farm asking for food and drink. The owner, warned to be on the look-out for the wanted man, suspected the caller might be Thornley and sent for the police. Officers hurried to the farm and made the arrest.

Thornley appeared at Macclesfield Borough Magistrates' Court on the following day charged with the murder of Frances Johnson and was remanded in custody to appear at the next sitting of the Chester Assizes.

The trial took place at Chester on Monday 25th October, before Lord Coleridge, and at the advice of his defence counsel, Mr Trevor Lloyd KC, Thornley pleaded not guilty to the charge.

Prosecuting counsel, Mr R B Banks KC, produced several witnesses to Thornley's strange behaviour, and damning evidence was supplied by one Lily Hemshaw, the cashier at the local Picture Palace. She knew both Thornley and the deceased well, and they had visited the 'Palace' together on many occasions.

On Thursday 16th September, the day before the murder, she had seen Frances in a dishevelled state, and enquired of Thornley what had happened. He was angry because Frances had pawned the engagement ring he had given her. 'I feel like doing her in,' he told the cashier, 'I will swing for her!'

Further evidence was supplied by Emma Wrigley, a widow, of Hayes Yard, King Street, Macclesfield. On 17th September, Thornley had visited her at home, with a framed photograph of himself which he asked her to keep. He was annoyed, he told her, as he had planned to go the theatre, but 'that plaguey little thing had got there first'. He was clearly referring to Frances, and Mrs Wrigley told him not to worry as there would be plenty of other seats in the theatre. He then added that he had been round to Frances's house on the previous evening and given Frances 'what her father daren't do'.

From the testimony of May Warren, it was established that Thornley had attempted to strangle Frances on that Thursday evening, an incident which resulted in May Warren again staying at the house on the night of the murder. Prosecution then produced two letters: one found at the scene of the murder was addressed to Frances's parents. It read:

> Dear Ma and Pa,
> I told you I would have killed or cured Frances and I have done it. I hope you will forgive me for breaking God's holy law.

The second letter, addressed to Mrs Emma Wrigley, had been drawn to the attention of the police by William Mullins, a baker, who had premises on Buxton Road. Giving evidence, he recalled:

'I was working in the bakehouse at 11 pm, on Friday 17th September. Thornley came in for a chat and left a few minutes later. He came back again at just before 3 o'clock on the Saturday morning and I asked him where on earth he was going at that time. He said he had a bit of extra work to do and he was going to do it. He gave me a letter, addressed to Mrs Wrigley, and asked me to post it for him. I agreed to do so and he left. He was perfectly rational at that time.'

This letter was then read out in court:

> Dear Ma,
> I went to see Frances but she was just in the same mind, so Ma,
> if you don't see me before Saturday, pray to God to forgive me

for what I have done. Go up to Calamine Street to my funeral as I want to be buried in Hurdsfield Church. God help us both and forgive us for what we have done. I told you I had done my best, and now I have done my worst.

Jack J. Thornley

Evidence was then heard from Dr Griffiths and Dr East, both of whom had observed Thornley whilst on remand. Both stated they had not seen any signs of insanity or homicidal mania in Thornley, nor was there anything written in the letters, nor in the way he had committed the murder, to suggest insanity. Both doctors spoke from vast experience of previous murderers and insanity.

Mr Trevor Lloyd KC, opening for the defence, wisely acknowledged the amount of evidence against the prisoner and said he declined to insult the intelligence and common sense of the jury with regard to the fact that Thornley had actually killed Frances Johnson. The issue now, he stated, was whether or not his client was insane at the time of the murder. With this in mind he called his first witness.

Mrs Elizabeth Thornley, of Calamine Street, mother of the accused, testified that her son had fits as a child. His brother had been killed three months before the murder and since then he had become very passionate and hasty. His outbursts would last a few minutes, then he would be normal again. He was irrational during these outbursts, once claiming that his mother should be in the pulpit at church or better still on the top of the steeple. His continuing strange behaviour caused her to ask him to leave the house. Closing her testimony, she added that Thornley's grandfather and two other relatives had been in an asylum. His behaviour had worsened since the break-up with Frances.

Two colleagues from the Hibel Road railway station, where Thornley was employed, stated that Thornley's behaviour had often been eccentric and they had previously questioned if he was 'altogether there'.

Summarising for the defence, Mr Lloyd asserted: 'Surely a sane man would not have behaved as Thornley did? If he was merely a cold-blooded killer, would he have gone round telling people he intended to "swing for" Frances? Would someone in his right mind have written the letters produced in evidence, which could only help put the rope around his neck? His behaviour at the canal was not that of a sane person. Having committed this awful murder, could it not be that he intended to commit suicide? Normal people do not go to a canal with the intention of killing themselves.'

31

Mr Lloyd closed by inviting the jury to consider the whole history of the case and to decide whether they thought Thornley was in full possession of his faculties or insane at the time of the murder.

This question was reiterated by Lord Coleridge in the summing-up. He advised the jury to take into account evidence of the prisoner's behaviour and family history, as it was a known medical fact that insanity could run in the family. Inability to control feelings or 'passions', however, was not an adequate reason to exonerate Thornley. By doing that, they would be saying that a man in a towering temper could be excused of a crime, because of his mood. Lord Coleridge also reminded them that the murder weapon had been placed in Frances's left hand. Was this done to suggest that Frances's wounds were self-inflicted? Medical evidence had already ruled out this possibility, so was it an attempt by Thornley to shift the blame elsewhere? That would give a sure guide as to whether he knew right from wrong. With this last point fresh in their minds, the jury retired to consider a verdict. They needed only 15 minutes to find Thornley guilty as charged. Lord Coleridge then sentenced Thornley to death. The whole proceeding had taken just six hours.

Under normal circumstances, Thornley would have been hanged at Knutsford Gaol which had taken over many years earlier from Chester Castle as the execution site for murders committed in Cheshire. However, in the summer of 1915, Knutsford Gaol had been taken over by the military, and the prisoner was therefore removed to Liverpool's Walton Gaol for execution. It was not without incident.

Thornley awaited his execution stoically. As the day drew closer he told his guards that he knew John Ellis the hangman. 'I saw him in Manchester once. I expect he will be the one to "do me in".' Destined to share the gallows with the Macclesfield murderer was a young American negro sailor named Young Hill, who had cut the throat of a fellow sailor on a ship moored off Liverpool's Canada Dock.

At 9 am, on Tuesday 1st December 1915, the two condemned men were led to the gallows. As Ellis strapped Thornley's wrists he couldn't fail to see the large tattoo on his lower arm. It was a large red heart with the name 'Frances' boldly picked out. Thornley took his place on the drop and with the rope around his neck he waited while Hill was made ready. As the American was noosed, he let out a fearful scream and began pleading to be spared. Unable to see what was happening, Thornley stood firm until the trapdoors crashed down and Frances Johnson was avenged.

5

'AFTER EASTER'

The Murders of Mrs Margaret Alderson Hodgson
and Miss Margaret Hodgson at Liscard
April 1917

My Dearest Helena,

Darling, I am worried to death about you because I think your mother mistrusts me. I shall not leave you in the cold, and if you have the patience to wait until after Easter we will make some arrangements, so don't worry. You will be all right with me before very long, and then I think we shall both be satisfied, and your mother too.

From your ever loving boy, Tom.

Thirty-four year old William Thomas ('Tom') Hodgson lived with his wife, son and daughter on Central Park Avenue, Liscard, Cheshire. Employed as a silk buyer for a Birkenhead drapery firm, he was well respected at work and by his neighbours, who looked upon him as a doting family man. But underneath the façade of domestic bliss, Hodgson was carrying on a relationship with a young waitress, an affair that had begun in the week after Easter, 1916.

Hodgson had moved to Liscard in 1915, after securing employment with Messrs Robb Bros. He was housed in temporary accommodation until, in the summer of 1916, he took possession of the house in Central Park Avenue, and brought his family over from their current home in Huddersfield.

Hodgson first met Helena Llewellyn, a pretty young waitress, when he became a frequent customer at the café where she worked, close to his office. One lunchtime he asked her out, she accepted, and within days they began a clandestine relationship.

Like any other couple they enjoyed romantic walks and frequent visits to the local cinema. Hodgson courted Helena attentively and they soon became lovers. On 21st March 1917, Helena discovered she was pregnant. On hearing this news, Hodgson assured Helena and her mother that all would be well and he would do right by the girl. He reaffirmed this in a letter, but asked her to be patient until 'after Easter' when he would make appropriate arrangements.

What Helena and her mother did not realise was that these 'arrangements', however appropriate they seemed to Hodgson, would not be to her advantage and would lead to a sensational murder trial just a few months later.

At 7.40 am on 16th April, next-door neighbour Mrs Eleanor Yates Law heard voices from the Hodgsons' back kitchen. She clearly heard the Hodgsons' young daughter Margaret (known as Metty) cry 'Don't do that', followed by her mother crying out 'Oh!' Then there was silence. At 8.30 am Tom Hodgson left for work.

Mrs Law knew that the Hodgsons frequently quarrelled, usually when Tom returned home after a drink, so she didn't pay much heed to the latest noise. She heard no further sounds from the house except for the intermittent crying of their baby son in his cot upstairs. The crying went on throughout the afternoon, and at 6 pm, she decided to call next door and check if all was well.

As it turned out, all was not well. After no one answered the door, which was unlocked, she let herself in and discovered the bloodied bodies of Mrs Hodgson and three year old Metty. The police were called and at 6.30 pm Chief Inspector Morris and Detective Inspector Pearson arrived at the house. The mother and daughter had been brutally murdered, the blood-spattered kitchen bearing witness to a terrible crime. Their heads had been viciously battered and a bloodstained hatchet lay between their bodies.

Dr Napier, the Wallasey police surgeon, arrived shortly afterwards and confirmed the nature of the deaths. Not only had they been battered to death, but several blows had been inflicted after death. Dr Napier established that the likely time of death was around 8 am, and from the half-cut loaf standing beside the sink, and the lack of food in the stomachs of the victims, the indications were that the killer had struck while Mrs Hodgson was preparing breakfast.

There were no signs of a struggle having taken place and it seemed the killer must have entered the house unseen and struck swiftly. However, police found no signs of a break-in or forced entry. It seemed

Central Park Avenue, Liscard.

that robbery was the motive, as an empty purse lay on the table alongside an empty money box. The robbery theory was further substantiated when police entered the front sitting room and found a large portmanteau packed with various items of silver, including a silver teapot, and a new set of tea knives.

The first thoughts were that the crimes might have been committed by a man whom Liverpool police were hunting in connection with a number of robberies known to have been carried out by someone who carried a hatchet. However, seasoned detectives felt sure that the thief – and murderer – they were looking for would not have failed to notice more expensive trinkets in the house which would have been the likely target for a 'professional thief'. Also, an experienced thief, even if he had been disturbed by a neighbour, would not have left the haul on the carpet as it was found. All in all, to the detectives at the scene, this suggested subterfuge.

The bloodstained hatchet was carefully moved from the floor and placed on the mantelpiece while the area was searched for further clues. An officer was dispatched to contact the murdered woman's husband at his place of employment, but Hodgson had left for home by the time police called at the works.

Tom Hodgson had left his office at the normal time and stopped off for a drink at the Charing Cross Hotel with a colleague, William Wilson. They enjoyed a drink and then Hodgson prepared to leave. 'Mustn't be late tonight, Bill,' he told his friend, 'the wife's off out to the cinema.'

Hodgson arrived home at 7.30 pm, to find his house swarming with police and an ambulance in attendance. Most of his neighbours also stood on their doorsteps watching events with a grim fascination.

'What's up here?' he asked the policeman at the door, forcing his way inside. Before he could be informed of the situation, Hodgson indicated the suitcase in the sitting room and proclaimed: 'Looks like something's wrong here, that's not mine!' He was also quick to spot the bloodstained axe on the mantelpiece and pointed out that it wasn't his. Up to that moment no mention had been made of the murder or murder weapon, but it seemed to the officers that Hodgson didn't seem surprised by what had happened and he quickly came under suspicion.

Hodgson was shown into the kitchen where he identified the bodies of his wife and daughter, and was then asked to accompany police to the local station to make a statement. Returning home after the interview with police, Hodgson reiterated his claim that the hatchet wasn't his and produced his own axe from the cupboard beneath the sink. After further investigations that night, Hodgson was formally cautioned and arrested for the murder of his wife. Angry neighbours hissed at him as he was led away by police.

William Thomas Hodgson stood trial before Mr Justice Avory at Chester Assizes on Wednesday 11th July 1917, charged with the murder of his wife and child. The courtroom was packed by curious locals eager to hear not only about the brutal murder but about the added scandal of Hodgson's extra-marital affair with the young waitress which had filled the local newspapers and offered a diversion from the horrors taking place in the war-torn fields of Europe.

Witnesses for the prosecution included Detective Inspector Pearson of the Wallasey police force who related the murder scene to the court, explaining where the bodies were found and the attempts to 'feign' a robbery.

Dr Napier gave medical evidence confirming the time and cause of death and further scientific evidence was provided by the brilliant Dr Bernard Spilsbury, medical adviser in criminal cases to the Home Office. Spilsbury had examined the clothes worn by Hodgson on the day of the murder and confirmed: 'There were bloodstains on the clothes, but although they were definitely from a mammal, I was unable to establish if they were human. They were recent stains, no more than one week old.' With blood-grouping still in its infancy, even the great Spilsbury was unable to be much help in this instance.

Mrs Eliza Godfrey, who lived opposite the Hodgsons, told the court how she had seen Hodgson as he left for work on that morning. 'He stopped twice to brush down his trousers, with his hand, and appeared to flick something off them,' she said in court.

Mrs Evelyn Carter, who sold fancy goods at Robb Bros, confirmed that two days before the murder, Hodgson had purchased a set of tea knives, which had formed part of the booty found in the portmanteau.

On the second day of the trial it was the turn of Helena Llewellyn to give evidence. The crowded court fell silent as she entered the witness box and took the oath. Helena told how she had met Hodgson, ironically just 'after Easter', in the previous year. She was unaware that he was married with two children and his attentions convinced her that he was truly in love with her. His interest waned somewhat by the Christmas of that year, but the relationship continued into 1917. It was in March that year, hearing of her pregnancy, that he had promised to do the right thing by her, both verbally and in writing. The 'Dearest Helena' letter was then read out aloud in court.

Miss Llewellyn reaffirmed that she knew nothing of Hodgson's existing domestic obligations, nor had he given her any indication as to what arrangements he proposed to make for them to be together.

Defending Hodgson, Mr Linden Riley rose and called the accused as his first witness. Despite being on trial for his life, Hodgson was calm as he entered the witness box, where in response to questions from Mr Riley he gave his account of the affair with Miss Llewellyn.

Hodgson confirmed that he had met her in a café and they had begun to see each other about twice a week. 'A few days after I first met her, an act of impropriety took place between us, and these acts continued until about March this year. I told her I was a married man in July 1916, during the first month of our acquaintance. Also in that month I showed her the house I had taken in Liscard, where I would live with my family from August of that year.'

Hodgson also confirmed that he had met with Miss Llewellyn and her mother in March 1917, because of Helena's condition, and agreed that he had promised to help her:

'I suppose her mother took it that I was going to marry the girl. The letter I wrote was with Helena's agreement, done for the purposes of misleading her mother, who did not know that I was a married man. I mentioned arrangements for "after Easter", as I had commission owed to me from Robb Bros., of £8 and 13 shillings.'

Hodgson denied that the idea of getting rid of his wife had even entered his head and stated that in their six years of marriage he had never so much as laid a finger on her. He admitted they had quarrelled occasionally about him taking a glass of beer, but that was all. They had slept in separate bedrooms since the fortnight before Easter, but this was on account of Metty's aversion to sleeping alone, not because of misunderstandings between him and his wife. He said he had parted from his wife and daughter on 16th April on perfectly affectionate terms.

Cross-examined by Mr Ellis Griffiths, for the prosecution, Hodgson explained that the bloodstains on his clothing were from a shaving cut shortly before the murder. He showed a total disregard for Helena Llewellyn's feelings by stating emphatically in court that he had never loved her and had no intention of marrying her, and even denied that he was the father of her illegitimate child. 'I had already tired of her by Christmas,' he stated.

It may be that Hodgson had spoken so coldly of Helena with a view to convincing the jury that he had planned no ill for his wife and child, but whatever his intentions, he emerged not only as a deceitful schemer, but as a cold, heartless one at that.

His defence counsel closed with the plea to the jury: 'Could the accused man really possess such a nerve as to murder his wife and child, go to work and about his business as usual, then calmly return home?' They took a little under 15 minutes to decide that he could.

Hodgson showed no emotion as Mr Justice Avory sentenced him to death. His appeal was unsuccessful and on Thursday 16th August 1917, he was hanged at Walton Gaol, Liverpool.

Why did William Hodgson murder his wife? In similar situations throughout the annals of crime, it is usually the mistress who pays with her life for burdening an adulterous husband with an unwanted offspring. If Hodgson really had no intention of leaving his wife, why did he cruelly beat her to death that spring morning? It was a secret he took with him to the gallows.

6

WITH MALICE AFORETHOUGHT?

The Murder of Ivy Wood at Hyde

July 1919

Friday 25th July 1919 had been eagerly anticipated by the workers at Carfield Cotton Mills, Hyde. It was the day of their annual works picnic, a trip to Blackpool, and the mill would be closed for the whole weekend. It was the first outing since before the War, but with grim coincidence, that weekend the silent machinery on the factory floor would witness a brutal rape and murder destined to make legal history.

Ivy Lydia Wood was pretty and intelligent. She was a promising swimmer, a fine singer, and at the age of 13, had much in life to look forward to. The daughter of a respected local businessman, Ivy was the apple of her father's eye and when she returned home from school that Friday afternoon, she was happy to run an errand for him. Ivy set off towards Mr Booth's store to buy the umbrella and walking-stick ferrules her father needed. It was the last time John Wood saw his daughter alive.

Earlier that afternoon, knowing that the mill would be empty for the weekend, the nightwatchman, 31 year old Arthur Beard, had seized the opportunity to treat himself to a couple of hours' unofficial drinking. Before starting his shift, which ran from 6 pm to 6 am, Beard had spent some time with his friend Charlie Jones in the Great War Comrades' Club.

As they parted company, Beard purchased a bottle of whisky to take out. They arranged to meet up again at 7 pm to attend a meeting of the Engine and Firemen's Union at the Navigation Hotel. Beard was keen to join the union and Jones took him along, hoping to put his name forward for membership. The meeting had ended at around 9 pm, and after another quick drink with his friend, Beard, by now having consumed a fair amount of drink, returned to work safe in the knowledge that his absence had not been noticed.

In the early hours of the following morning, Samuel Bower, a watchman at an adjacent mill, was roused from a nap by the frantic shouting of Arthur Beard. Seemingly drunk, Beard told him that he had found a girl in the grounds of his mill: 'I'm in a bit of a mess . . . I have found a girl pegged out . . . I was in the grounds near the dining room . . . I carried her back to the lodge.'

Bower followed Beard back to the mill and after confirming that there was indeed a body, he went to fetch a policeman. At 2 am PC Vernon accompanied Bower back to Carfield Mills and found the body of a young girl. She appeared to have been the victim of a violent assault: there was blood on her face and her clothing was dishevelled and covered in what looked like clay. The constable noted at once that Beard's trousers were also stained with clay around the knees and when he asked him how he had dirtied the trousers, Beard told him that he had slipped while carrying the girl back inside.

As more police descended on the mill, including the Chief Constable, Beard was again asked about the clay on his trousers. This time he said that he had fallen while patrolling near the mill pond. These changes in the story immediately aroused suspicion with the Hyde police and they detained Beard for further questioning.

On the following afternoon, local detectives were joined by officers from Scotland Yard in combing the extensive mill grounds for further clues. Chief Inspector Neil and Sergeant Evesleigh travelled up from London, and on searching the mill they soon found small but vital clues which pointed to the involvement of Arthur Beard. Tiles were splashed with blood, and matted in the blood was hair the same colour as Ivy's. Dirt on both Beard's and Ivy's clothing was similar to that in the cellar.

Inquiries amongst Ivy's family and friends established when Ivy was last seen and what she wearing. Ernest Gosling, a classmate of the dead girl, told police that he had seen her chatting to a man at the gates of Carfield Mills at teatime on the night she disappeared. Mr Booth, the ironmonger, also told police that he had sold Ivy the ferrules she had requested. These ferrules were now missing, as was the hair ribbon Ivy had worn that afternoon.

The evidence against Arthur Beard was mounting, but detectives were not yet in a position to charge him. They needed a breakthrough soon, as he could not be held indefinitely and his lawyer was already

Ivy Lydia Wood.

pressing officers to 'charge or release him'. They were unable to do the former and disinclined to do the latter, the pitiful sight of Ivy's battered body on the mortuary slab having strengthened their resolve to bring the killer to justice.

It was something of a surprise, therefore, when in the later hours of Sunday 27th July Arthur Beard confessed to the murder and signed a statement to that effect:

'I had been drinking. I knew the little girl, and as we chatted on Friday 25th July at 6 pm, I invited her into the mill. I don't know what possessed me to do it, but I pulled her onto my knee. We struggled and I put my hand over her mouth. I must have fallen asleep, and when I awoke I saw her body lying in the room in front of me. It was cold and stiff, so I lifted it up in my arms, carried it through the mill and threw it

42

Carfield Cotton Mills, Hyde.

over onto the waste ground.'

On the Monday morning, Carfield Mills reopened and shocked workers were asked to search the shop floor for anything unusual. Within the hour, Ivy's hair ribbon and the three umbrella ferrules were found by operatives searching near their machines.

In October 1919, Arthur Beard stood trial for his brutal crime at Cheshire Assizes before Mr Justice Bailache. He was charged with the murder of Ivy Lydia Wood, and it was alleged that whilst attempting to commit rape, he had suffocated her.

In his defence, it was asserted that Beard was drunk and that, as his mind was impaired by drink, the crime should be reduced from wilful murder to manslaughter – the difference between life and death if he was convicted.

Attempting to clarify the position to the jury, Mr Justice Bailache told the jury that a verdict of manslaughter could be returned only if his drunkenness had made him unaware of what he was doing, or unaware that what he was doing was wrong.

After a lengthy amount of legal argument and cross-examination of witnesses, the jury took only a short time to consider their verdict before returning to find Beard guilty as charged. The three-day trial ended with the judge sentencing Beard to death.

Arthur Beard.

Despite admitting his guilt, Beard was not about to go to the scaffold without a fight, and his counsel immediately launched an appeal against conviction. Again, their plea was: 'How could Beard have formed the intention to kill if he was so intoxicated?' To be convicted of murder the prisoner would have had to show 'malice aforethought', and that had not been shown in Beard's case. Defence counsel also cited the judge as having misdirected the jury during his summing-up.

To the surprise of many of those present, the appeal was successful and the verdict of murder was reduced to one of manslaughter. The death sentence was then commuted to life imprisonment with a recommendation that he serve 20 years.

In Hyde, and elsewhere across the country, public opinion was outraged. Ignoring the technicalities of the legal system, they found it hard to be lenient to Arthur Beard. Were they to accept that Beard should not pay the ultimate penalty for the rape and murder of a 13 year old child, if her death was merely the by-product of his heinous violation?

Spurred on by the public outcry, Sir Gordon Hewatt KC, the Director of Public Prosecutions, lodged an unprecedented further appeal to the House of Lords, objecting to the reduction in sentence. The Bar assembled to hear this further appeal included some of the most eminent Law Lords of the day, including the Lord Chancellor, the Lord Chief Justice and two former Lord Chancellors.

The hearing took three days, between 16th and 19th December 1919, but it was to be almost three months before the result of the appeal was announced:

> The jury at the trial had no actual evidence that Beard had been drunk at all. There had certainly been no evidence that he was too drunk to form the intent of committing rape. Under the circumstances, it was proved that death was caused by an act of violence done in the furtherance of the felony of rape and, that by English Law, such killing is murder.

News that the original verdict had been reinstated was met with indifference by Beard. He had already been advised that regardless of the outcome of the second appeal he would not hang, and that instead his sentence would remain at life imprisonment. This was, indeed, the outcome. It was felt that the to-ing and fro-ing of verdicts had caused Beard 'mental anguish'. In any event, a surprisingly merciful attitude was shown to the callous and brutal killer who had violated and murdered such an innocent young girl on that fateful midsummer's evening in 1919.

7

'THE GREED OF GOLD'

The Murder of Margaret Gilchrist White at Bramhall

December 1922

The role of the jury has been an integral part of the British legal system since the 12th century. Derived from the French *juré*, meaning sworn, a jury originally consisted of a body of men assembled together to meet the visiting Assize judges who travelled into various parts of the country to try important cases.

The original role of the jury was to bring the accused to trial, by whatever means necessary. Thus, the prisoner's fate was usually decided by 'trial by ordeal', which often meant having a confession forced out of them by 'the third degree'. By the 15th century, a jury had independence from the Government and judiciary and henceforth a body of 12 men (women only began to serve at murder trials in 1921) was sworn to decide points of fact based on the available evidence and to be directed where necessary on points of law by the judge. A verdict had to be unanimous and it was not until as late as 1967 that majority verdicts were permitted.

One of the major difficulties facing a jury, usually comprising lower- or working-class folk whose grasp of common law was negligible, was that a good counsel could easily baffle them. Imagine, then, the difficulties facing them when the trial lacked the usual abundance of evidence from witnesses to the actual crime, or when the accused exhibited any strange behaviour, or when there was no conclusive medical or forensic evidence. In cases such as these, the scales of justice were tipped by opposing arguments from defence and prosecution counsel, and when these were presented by brilliant legal minds, each version of events could sound as plausible as the next. This was the quandary facing the jury at Chester Assizes in March 1923,

94 Acre Lane, Bramhall.

when a former soldier stood trial for murder.

Frederick George Wood was born in Bradford in 1893. He served his country well during the First World War until he was invalided out of the Northumberland Fusiliers in November 1917. Although granted a small army pension, in order to make ends meet he travelled the country working as an upholsterer, staying in cheap boarding houses and taking pot-luck by calling from door to door in search of jobs.

Fortune appeared to smile on Fred Wood when, on the morning of Monday 18th December 1922, he raised the heavy brass door knocker at 'Invermay', 94 Acre Lane, Bramhall, and his request for work was greeted in the affirmative.

No 94 Acre Lane, a pleasant 'villa'-style house set back off the road, was the home of 50 year old spinster Miss Margaret Gilchrist White and her brother John, a bank clerk who worked for the London County Westminster Bank in Manchester. Whilst by no means an invalid, Miss White did not keep the best of health and until recently had employed a live-in housekeeper to help run the home. Early in December, the housekeeper had left and a replacement had yet to be found.

Miss White was last seen at around 9.15 on the morning of 18th

December, when a postman saw her as he delivered a letter at the house. Two hours later her next-door neighbour heard the sound of hammering coming from the house, but when a young girl called at around at 4.30 pm to deliver some eggs, she received no reply.

John White usually returned home at 6 pm, but this day he had to see someone in Manchester and caught the later train, arriving home at 7 pm. As he approached the door he was surprised to find the house in darkness. He let himself in and noticed immediately that the kitchen had been ransacked.

He lit the gas and on entering the dining room stumbled over the body of his sister. It was clear that Margaret was dead. She was lying on her back with her hands tied together and resting against her throat. She was fully clothed although her apron, the string of which bound Miss White's hands, had been pulled up to cover her face. In the front sitting room, whining pitifully, was the family dog Bruno, who had probably been locked in there while Miss White answered the front door.

The police were called and a search was made of the house. In the upstairs bedroom the contents of the dressing-table drawers were emptied on the floor and several metal cashboxes had been forced open. It seemed that the killer had been searching for cash only, as a gold watch and other items of jewellery lay untouched on the dressing table. It was thought that some two or three pounds had been inside the metal boxes, all of which showed clear fingerprint impressions. Lying on the bedroom floor was a length of webbing of the sort used to repair chairs.

Late in the evening, Dr Thompson carried out a post-mortem and estimated the time of death as around noon that day. It is perhaps strange to note that although the victim's hands had been bound together, it was at first thought that death may have been due to natural causes. This theory seems to have been based on the knowledge that Miss White suffered from a weak heart; but further examination revealed that death was due to strangulation.

There was no sign of a forced entry and the crime did not seem to have been a carefully planned exercise, as the killer had made little effort to cover his tracks. John White told police that there was a chair standing in the hall which had not been there when he left for work. The chair had been stripped down for reupholstering. Other clues lying around the house pointed to the involvement of a furniture repairer.

The most important clue left at the scene was a business card bearing

Frederick George Wood and Detective Inspector Kingham arrive at court in Chester.

a name and address: Fred Wood 'Up-holsterer', c/o Mrs Cooper, Church Street, Wilmslow. Officers called at the house but found that Wood had apparently left the area several days earlier.

A description of the wanted man, who also went under the name of Ronald Lee, was issued, depicting him as: 'Aged 29 years; 5 feet 7 inches tall; clean shaven; last seen wearing a light tweed suit, light-coloured cap; blue collar and tie; black army boots'. Wood was also said to have gunshot wounds on his left arm and tattoos on his chest; a wanted poster carrying his picture appeared outside police stations across the country. It was known that the wanted man frequented many lodging houses in and around Wilmslow, but a search of these and others in the county failed to locate him.

On the day following the murder, Chief Inspector Brown travelled up from Scotland Yard to liaise with Superintendent Ludlow and Inspector Kingham who had been assigned to the case. Investigations continued around the county without much success, and although several men were taken into custody for further questioning, all were later released without charge.

It was something of a surprise when on Saturday morning, 23rd December, word reached the murder headquarters that a man had been detained at Lincoln police station regarding this investigation.

Inspector Kingham travelled to Lincoln and spoke to the man, who gave his name as Fred Wood. Wood said that he had called at the police station with regard to the murder inquiry after seeing his picture on the wanted notice. He admitted doing some work for Miss White but strenuously denied murdering her. On Christmas morning, 1922, Wood was formally charged with the wilful murder of Miss White and was remanded for trial at the Assizes.

Mr Justice Rigby Swift presided over events when Wood stood in the dock at Chester on 1st March 1923. There now began a legal battle with enough twists to confuse even the most astute of juries.

Sir Ellis Griffiths KC led for the Crown and outlined the prosecution case to the jury. Miss White's body was found in a downstairs room at her house. Upstairs in the bedroom were a number of opened and empty cashboxes bearing Wood's fingerprints. A strip of webbing found on the bedroom floor matched webbing used by Wood at another house in Bramhall earlier that month. Wood was also seen by a witness walking towards the house at 10.40 am on the day of the murder, and it was found that he had caught the 12.30 pm Bramhall to Stockport bus.

Leading for the defence, Mr Goodman Roberts KC first referred to the statement Wood had made shortly after his arrest in which he claimed to have walked from the house after repairing the chair, and to have caught the 11.30 am bus to Stockport. This would put him well away from the house at noon, when it was firmly established that the murder took place.

When it was found that several witnesses contradicted this statement, the defence put forward a suggestion that whilst Wood may have contributed to Miss White's death, this was accidental, and the charge at worst should be manslaughter.

In a statement made shortly before being charged with the murder, Wood gave a version of what had happened in the house that morning. He said that he had been repairing a chair and was chatting with Miss White when she suddenly became ill. 'She grasped at her throat and collapsed,' he said, adding that when he saw that she had passed out, he panicked. Wood said he was scared that no one would believe the truth and he had then ransacked the house looking for money to help him flee the area. He added that some of the money he took was owed to him for repairing the chair! He said that he had tied her hands with the apron strings so that if she had come round while he was in the house she wouldn't have been able to raise the alarm.

Challenging the suggestion that Wood had strangled Miss White, his counsel referred to the shrapnel wound in his left arm and said that he had insufficient strength in his injured arm to cause strangulation. This was countered by Sir Ellis Griffiths, who pointed out the strength needed by Wood to get enough tension in the webbing when reupholstering chairs.

As the evidence unfolded, it seemed clear that there were two distinct opinions on what had happened that day. It was an undisputed fact that Wood was in the house at some time that morning, but what were the jury to believe? Did they believe the prosecution's version of events, that Wood committed murder during the course of robbery; or the defence's version, that Miss White died of natural causes?

'If the accused had intended to commit robbery, surely he would have stolen the watch and jewellery,' Mr Roberts told the jury, concluding his case. 'There are two great questions involved here,' he said. 'Was Miss White murdered at all, and if she was, did the prisoner murder her? If you are not satisfied that Miss White was murdered, if you believe she died a natural death, then that is the end of the case. If you think she died a death which was not fully natural, but was contributed to by ill-advised conduct, carelessness or callousness, and not by a criminal act, then there was no murder.'

Sir Ellis Griffiths closed his case by pointing to the clear motive for the murder. 'Do you know a greater motive for murder in the world than the greed of gold?' he asked the jury as he ended his address.

Summing up the case, Mr Justice Swift made the observation that there were many women in the country who had to be left alone during the day while their menfolk went to work, and such people should be protected. It seemed clear which version of events the judge felt was correct, and less than one hour later the jury returned to find Wood guilty of murder, adding a strong recommendation for mercy. The three-day trial ended with sentence of death passed in the usual manner.

An appeal before the Lord Chief Justice was heard at the end of March, based on the fact that the trial judge had not allowed the jury to consider a verdict of manslaughter. Listening to the appeal, the panel concurred with the findings at the original trial and said that the only proper verdicts on the evidence were guilty or an acquittal.

Despite the recommendation for mercy and several petitions launched on his behalf, Fred Wood was hanged at Walton Gaol, Liverpool, on 10th April 1923.

8

THE
PUBLIC CHASTISER

The Murder of Percy Sharpe at Northenden
September 1923

At 14 years of age Percy Sharpe was another one of thousands of school-leavers who, in the summer of 1923, joined the growing list of the unemployed. The boom time the economy had enjoyed following the First World War was gradually coming to an end and the country was slowly but surely slipping into a severe depression.

For the Sharpe family at their home on South Street, Ardwick, Manchester, times were especially hard. When his father had to give up work with rheumatic fever, Percy, the eldest of four children, took it upon himself to act as the breadwinner, a position he took very seriously despite his youth.

At 8 o'clock on the morning of Tuesday 4th September 1923, Percy was getting ready for the first of his twice-weekly visits to the Juvenile Labour Exchange on Albert Square. He finished his breakfast, checked his appearance in the hall mirror, pocketed his diary and labour card, and bidding his parents good morning, set out on his journey.

Joining the long queue, Percy greeted one of his former classmates before getting into a conversation with an older man who was loitering in the building as if waiting for someone. After signing for his money, Percy and the man walked outside together, whereupon the man told Percy that he knew where there was some work going, and if he would meet him on Oxford Road later that morning, he promised to help Percy get a job. Desperate for any kind of job, Percy accepted the offer.

At 2.30 that afternoon, signalman James Edwards, at his post manning the box at Northenden Junction, was preparing for the passing of a Manchester-bound express train, when his attention was

53

taken by what he first thought was a young girl in a red dress, crossing the footbridge away from Carr's Wood. Once the train had passed, Edwards looked out again and saw to his horror that what he took to be a girl in a red dress, was in fact a young boy, naked from the waist down, bleeding from a horrific chest wound.

Platelayer James Hetherington had been working on the railway line when he had heard someone screaming. He walked down the line past Carr's Wood, and seeing the young boy on the footbridge, he hurried onward.

'Come quickly, I am dying,' the young boy cried as he collapsed to the ground.

'What's happened, lad?' Hetherington asked as he was joined by the signalman.

'A man has stabbed me, up yonder,' the boy moaned, indicating towards the woods.

'Do you know who did it?' he was asked. He replied that he didn't, but was able to give a brief description of his attacker.

Hetherington, seeing the gaping wound in the boy's chest, told Edwards to run to nearby Northenden station and call the police, while he picked up the boy in his arms and carried him across the street to the adjacent Rose Hill Ophthalmic School, where Nurse Eastman tended to his wounds until an ambulance arrived.

While waiting for the ambulance, the nurse questioned the boy about his attack. He gave his name as Percy Sharpe and said he had met a man that morning while signing on, and at the man's promise of a job, he had met up with him again on Oxford Road shortly before dinner. They then took a tram to Alexander Park, Whalley Range, alighting at the Palatine Road terminus. Next they took a bus to Northenden. Percy then said that after the man had bought him a ginger beer he took him into the woods where he attempted to assault him. When he resisted, the man stabbed him in the chest.

With a faltering voice and grimacing with pain as he tried to speak, Percy weakly dictated what happened: 'Came from Manchester with me. Oxford Road. Promised me work. He did it with a knife. Wiped it on the grass and put it in his pocket. Came by bus about dinner time to Northenden and then walked to the woods . . . I didn't know the man.' Asked to describe his attacker, he said he was clean shaven, wore a check cap and mackintosh, and was middle aged.

Officers from the Cheshire Constabulary rushed to the school, where Sergeant Ted Furness questioned Percy about his attacker. After being repeatedly asked to describe his assailant, Percy closed his eyes, rolled onto his side and pleaded: 'Shut up!'

Dr Hardman was summoned from his surgery close by, and after dressing the boy's wounds he took him by motor car to Stockport Infirmary. The doctor told the police as they left that he didn't hold out much hope for the boy's chances of surviving the journey, but they made it to the hospital and Percy was rushed into theatre for an urgent operation.

Surgeons found that Percy had been stabbed in the abdomen; the wound had pierced the stomach wall, damaging the liver and causing massive internal bleeding. The youngster survived the operation but his condition worsened and with his parents at his bedside, Percy Sharpe died from his injuries at 5 am the next day.

While Percy was being tended to at Rose Hill Ophthalmic School, officers began to search the area where he had been attacked. PC Sam Jones found a bundle of clothes less than 100 yards from Northenden station. These included Percy's overcoat, jacket, waistcoat and cap. The jacket's sleeves were still inside the overcoat, suggesting that they had been pulled off together. There was no sign of the boy's trousers, underpants and braces, but close by were three patches of blood a few inches apart. The area was cordoned off as scores of officers combed the area for further clues, hampered in parts by the thick undergrowth.

Residents on Northenden Road, Gatley, the closest houses to Carr's Wood, were interviewed, and while many recollected hearing screams from the wood, nobody saw anyone or anything untoward.

The first witness to say she had seen Percy and his killer was Mrs Pearson, a fruit seller with a stall on Gatley Road. She told police that a man and a boy stopped by her stall and the lad asked for some fruit, but the man wouldn't buy anything. Her description was similar to that given by Percy Sharpe; she said the man was in his fifties, with red cheeks; he was clean shaven and had a smiling expression.

On the following day a young boy playing out in Chorlton found a knife which police indicated might be the murder weapon. It was the first vital piece of evidence, but an even bigger breakthrough came on Friday evening, 7th September.

Detective Inspector Kingham was *en route* to Barnes Hospital to follow up a lead when he spotted a man talking to a group of young boys. His description matched that of the killer on every count and Kingham stopped to question him. The man said his name was David Colthorpe and gave his address as a lodging house on Canal Street,

Stockport. Colthorpe was aged around 45 and when Kingham searched his lodgings, he found traces of blood on his suit. Colthorpe told the officer that he couldn't remember what he had done on the day of the murder but he was sure he was at home at the time.

The knife found at Chorlton was shown to other lodgers at the house and a number said it resembled a knife Colthorpe owned. Evidence began to mount against Colthorpe. It was learned from his friends that he spent a lot of time mixing with young boys, often buying them sweets and taking them for walks. One friend told the Inspector that after reading in the paper about the murder, Colthorpe had turned to him and said: 'I've done nothing to any children around here. Go and ask them!' It had seemed an unusual thing for someone to say and Inspector Kingham thought so too, as he took the statement.

Colthorpe's guilt seemed even more certain to the detectives when he was placed in an identity parade of 17 men and immediately picked out by Mrs Pearson, the fruit seller. Several other witnesses, including Percy's friends from the Labour Exchange, were not quite so sure and failed to pick him out. Nevertheless, convinced that he had his man, Inspector Kingham charged Colthorpe with the murder of Percy Sharpe and had him remanded in Strangeways Prison.

Between Colthorpe's incarceration and his scheduled appearance at the police court, several pieces of new evidence came in to support his protestations of innocence. First, investigations found that despite Colthorpe failing to remember where he was at the time of the murder, it now transpired that he was signing on at Stockport Labour Exchange, and several witnesses swore to this effect. Second, the blood found on Colthorpe's clothing, while identified as human blood, was discovered when analysed by a Home Office expert to predate the murder and had probably been in place for several weeks. Also Colthorpe's boots, the only pair he owned, were very shabby and well worn, unlike the stout, polished black boots Percy recalled that his attacker had been wearing.

All this evidence was presented before a jury at Withington police court a few weeks later and the hearing ended with the jury finding that Percy Sharpe was wilfully murdered by a person or persons unknown. David Colthorpe was then discharged and walked from the court a free man.

The case remained in the headlines and speculation that the killer may have been an escapee from a nearby lunatic asylum soon changed when the body of a man was found on the railway line, less than 100 yards from the Northenden Junction signal box, and almost adjacent to the spot where young Percy was murdered. Was this a case of the suicide of someone riddled with guilt and remorse?

The dead man was identified as 47 year old Stethill Mattinson, a Manchester fire surveyor. A number of people who had identified Colthorpe on the parade were invited to the mortuary to see if this man seemed familiar. As before, a number thought he looked like the man. Police suspicions were further aroused when a check through the man's papers found contradictory writings in his diary. The entry on the day of the murder showed that he was to meet up with a man in Oldham, but when police checked this out, they found that Mattinson had not kept this appointment.

The mystery of the suicide was soon cleared up though when investigations found that Mattinson was in dire financial straits and had a number of pressing debts, for which creditors were starting to get impatient. A heavy drinker, Mattinson had taken to the bottle and chose to end his life in the path of a passing express train.

Exactly four months to the day after the murder, police got their man. A number of reports had reached Inspector Kingham that a man had been terrorising young boys in Alexander Park, Whalley Range, Manchester. The man, it seemed, had taken it upon himself to inflict punishments on young boys whom he had caught cycling or smoking in the park. Irate parents had told police that the man was alleged to have struck their children with his belt or clipped them around the ear with his hand.

On 4th January 1924, Police Constable Lawrence was sent to investigate and spotted a man chasing a group of young boys away from the park. Lawrence caught up with the man and questioned him about his activities. The man gave his name as Francis Wilson Booker, a 28 year old unemployed warehouseman, and an address at a lodging house on nearby Carter Street.

Lawrence's initial thoughts were that Booker, with a crop of grey hair, looked much older than his 28 years. He was taken to the nearby police station and asked to empty his pockets. Inside were five notebooks chronicling punishments and beatings which the self-styled 'public chastiser' had handed out to youngsters in the previous months. Booker was identified by a number of children whose parents had made a complaint to the police, and as a result he was held on four counts of assault, which he admitted.

Four days later, with Booker on remand, officers searched his room at the lodging house. Booker shared a front bedroom with two other lodgers, and looking through his possessions they came across a black suitcase which contained three pairs of boy's trousers. Then came the breakthrough. Inside this case was a diary and labour card both of which bore the name Percy Sharpe.

A further search of the house found another pair of boy's trousers, hidden in the cellar, to which Booker had access. These were badly torn and appeared to have been washed. His landlady told police that Booker also had an allotment on Princess Road, next to Alexander Park, and close to where Percy said he had been taken by his killer. Inside a greenhouse police found a pair of bloodstained braces which, along with the torn trousers, were shown to Percy's parents. Mrs Sharpe broke down in tears as she pointed out the stitching with which she had repaired the trousers.

Three days after finding the clothing in Booker's rooms, Superintendent Tonge, who had taken charge of the investigation, questioned the prisoner. Booker repeatedly denied any involvement in the murder but when the diary, labour card and braces were placed on the table before him, he began to shake and his lips quivered.

'I found them in a parcel,' he said, after being told they had been discovered in his possession. Asked why he hadn't reported it to the police, Booker claimed he was scared that he might fall under suspicion if he did so. Satisfied that they finally had their man, the police charged Booker with the wilful murder of Percy Sharpe.

Mr Justice Greer presided over the trial at Manchester Assizes which opened on 26th February. It was to be the first major murder trial at Manchester since the same judge had sent Frederick 'Eric' Holt, the infamous St Anne's murderer, to the gallows four years before, and the court was packed as proceedings opened.

Mr Wingate Saul KC led for the prosecution and highlighted the Crown's case. Items identified as belonging to the murdered boy had been found in Booker's possession, and several witnesses, from the boy's parents to textile experts, corroborated this fact.

The prosecution called two young boys who testified that they had been with Booker at various times to Carr's Wood, and one said that on the last visit Booker had suggested an indecent act. The boy said he had run away.

Fellow lodgers at the Carter Street lodgings told that Booker had grown a beard shortly after the murder; until this time he had always been clean shaven. Press reports which said that police were looking

Francis Booker.

for a man who was clean shaven were found amongst Booker's belongings.

Wingate Saul then produced the diaries found in Booker's pocket when arrested. Listed against the 'punishments' Booker had handed out were the initials: 'NBK' and 'GK'. Booker admitted that these letters stood for navy blue knickers and grey knickers. Booker was also asked why the pages referring to 4th September 1923 were missing from his diary. He could offer no explanation for this.

When asked why there were three pairs of boy's underpants found in his room, Booker said that he stolen one pair from a washing line, taken one from a rag and bone cart and found a third pair on the local tip. In closing, Saul asked whether it was just a coincidence that the only items missing from the murder scene were Percy's trousers, underpants and braces.

On the second day the defence called Booker into the dock. He seemed to hurry forward, and picking up the Bible to take the oath, he kissed it fervently. He claimed that the items belonging to Percy Sharpe, found in his possession, had been discovered while he was out cycling close to Carr's Wood. Booker said that he found the package in the road and took it home without opening it. He had forgotten about the bundle until nearly two months later, when he came across it whilst tidying up. He claimed he couldn't remember hiding it in the cellar.

Cross-examining the prisoner, Wingate Saul asked Booker if he had admitted to Superintendent Tonge that he had been frightened when he found the clothing belonged to the murdered boy. Booker denied saying this.

Mr Kenneth Burke KC, Booker's counsel, in closing the defence, told the jury that they should acquit the prisoner, as in his mind it was clear there was no actual evidence that Booker had committed the murder. He pointed to the evidence of Mrs Pearson, who had identified David Colthorpe as the man seen with Percy on that fateful day. She had also thought that the suicide victim resembled Percy's accomplice. It was strange, then, Burke told the jury, that she had failed to pick out Booker at an identity parade. Booker, he also pointed out, did not fit the description given by several witnesses who had seen Percy that morning. 'Surely, if my client was guilty, he would have burned the incriminating evidence rather than leave it lying around where it could easily be found?' Burke asked in a last desperate plea.

The jury took just 25 minutes to find Booker guilty as charged and Mr Justice Greer sentenced him to be hanged. Watching from the gallery as Booker walked nonchalantly from the dock was David Colthorpe.

An appeal, that the judge had misdirected the jury on certain points, was heard at the Appeal Court in London. It was quickly rejected and Booker was returned to the condemned cell at Manchester to await execution.

The hangman selected to carry out the execution was William Willis who had been promoted to chief executioner a few weeks previously. Curiously enough, Willis lived less than a mile from the man who was to be his third 'customer'.

The condemned man received just one visitor whilst awaiting the hangman. His elderly father travelled up from Booker's home town of Horncastle, Lincolnshire, to see his son. The old man was perplexed that his only son, who had medals for bravery awarded during the Great War, could have changed into a perverted killer.

Willis watched Booker at exercise and recorded that he ate like a horse, smoked like a chimney and seemed to have no fear of his imminent demise. On Tuesday 8th April 1924, Francis Wilson Booker was hanged at Strangeways Prison, Manchester. Hundreds of people gathered at the prison gates, many of them women who wept when the notice was posted to show that the Carr's Wood killer had paid the full penalty.

9

THE
FAVOURITE DAUGHTER

The Murder of Louise Leah at Over Alderley
September 1926

In many Cheshire farming communities in the early part of the 20th century, the head of the household was, appropriately enough, also the breadwinner of the family. Hard work, sweat and toil, prerequisites of life on the land, were repaid by the farmer's family with love, obedience and due respect. This situation prevailed in most families at that time and proving no exception was the Leah family of Finlow Hill Farm, Over Alderley, near Wilmslow.

At 60 years of age, James Leah was a giant of a man, an imposing figure with a thick black beard, and whilst he was a hard-working farmer and family man, the lines between discipline and dominance had become blurred, and his family lived in fear of this quick-tempered, overbearing patriarch. His wife had left him many times on account of his bullying, and the three children who remained at home, Louise, Elsie and John, had learned to live with the turbulent, quarrelsome atmosphere.

The Leahs' eldest son had emigrated to Australia some five years previously, and their eldest daughter Margaret had lived at nearby Dickens Farm since her marriage seven years earlier. Her husband was also a hard-working farmer, but James Leah, always difficult to please, did not approve of him, so Margaret had not visited the family home since her wedding.

By the late summer of 1926, the atmosphere at Finlow Farm had become unbearable and on 9th September, young John Leah told his father that 'unless there were different goings on', he would leave. The situation remained as it was and true to his word, on 11th September, John packed his things and left for good.

Maybe the lack of another male presence at the farm unnerved Mrs Leah, but whatever the reason, on Friday 24th September, following a row on the previous evening, she and her two daughters agreed to leave. They ate a last breakfast together before Mrs Leah left.

James Leah asked Louise where her mother had gone. 'Up to the woods,' she replied, not wishing to provoke his temper. He was no fool, however, and smelled a conspiracy. 'This is a planned job,' he said, following Elsie out to the milking shed. Father and daughter then quarrelled and returning to the kitchen, Elsie stated quite bluntly that she too was moving out that day.

As Elsie was driven away in a taxi, 20 year old Louise was left to placate their father. Because of her more placid nature, she was her father's favourite, but instead of this assuring her safety, by 12.30 that afternoon she was only two hours from death, staggering to her sister Margaret at nearby Dickens Farm, with blood gushing from a wound to her neck.

Margaret was horrified at the sight of her wounded sister, who had a gash to the back of her neck so deep that it had almost cut off her scalp, and the police were quickly called. They hurried to Finlow Farm on the advice of Margaret, and found James Leah lying in a fodder bin, covered with hay. He had a knife wound in his throat but was still able to confess his actions to the police. 'I did her in the kitchen with the hedge cutter. I cut myself with this knife and came here to finish it off. She's the best girl I've got – I couldn't bear her to go. My poor Louise.'

Leah was placed under arrest by Detective Inspector Wakelin and Sergeant Barber, and taken to the Cottage Hospital, where under the supervision of Dr Buchanan, he was given medical attention. He seemed confused and told Superintendent Kingham, of Chester Constabulary, who had taken charge of the investigations: 'I'm no scholar, to understand anything. Did I tell you something? Has there been a death?'

'Yes,' Supt. Kingham replied. 'Louise is dead.'

Leah was stunned. 'I would have parted with anybody rather than that girl.'

This sentiment was reiterated for the jury at Chester Assizes on Wednesday 17th October 1926. Mr Justice Fraser presided over the trial, which saw James Leah accused of the wilful murder of his daughter.

Defence counsel, Mr Dallas Walters, realised the futility of trying to show that Leah had not killed his daughter, and concentrated his case on the issue of 'intent'. He explained this to the jury: 'James Leah was a

Finlow Hill Farm, Over Alderley, under renovation in 1996.

man under immense pressure. Solely responsible for the running of the farm, he worried how he would cope when his wife left him on the morning of Friday 24th September. He had a poor relationship with his daughter Elsie, as he did not approve of her boyfriend, and the anguish he felt at the prospect of being abandoned by both her and Louise drove him into a frenzy.'

Leah himself was called as a witness for the defence and he looked a pathetic figure in the dock. He spoke quietly, suppressing his emotions, and said: 'I asked Louie on that Friday was she leaving me too? She said "Yes" and I begged her "Don't go, Louie, stay here with me", but she just answered me snappily. I had no intention of killing Louie or of doing her any grievous bodily harm. I wasn't.responsible. I was that weighed down with trouble because the mother and all had gone.'

Leah then broke down and there were few in the courtroom unmoved by this tragic tale and the sight of the distraught farmer.

Cross-examined by Mr Bertram Long, for the prosecution, Leah denied that he had a violent temper but admitted that this was not the first time he had flown into a frenzy of rage.

Medical opinion on Leah's mental state was offered by Dr Ahearn,

Senior Medical Officer at Walton Gaol, where the prisoner had been held on remand. He told the court: 'Although I found no evidence of mental disease in the prisoner, he labours under delusions. There are also signs of emotional weakness, which can be attributed to mental deterioration. I would say he is a man prone to emotional excitement, which may often take the form of anger. During the first stages of these outbursts, he would not be fully conscious of the results of his actions, nor the purpose he had in view. After a short time, he would realise what he had done and then be filled with remorse.'

Questioned by Mr Long, Dr Ahearn confirmed that he had failed to find evidence of any definite mental disease in the accused. This effectively discounted the possibility of a defence of insanity, and Leah, who looked like a broken man, sat with his head sunk into his chest throughout the judge's summing-up.

The jury retired to consider its verdict and returned exactly one hour later. Based on the hard facts of the case, there could be no other verdict than 'guilty', but for the tragic man whose misguided love and fear of loneliness had caused him to destroy what he treasured most, the jury offered a recommendation of mercy. Whether this would have been in reality a mercy to James Leah will never be known. In remorse for the death of Louise, or 'Louie' as he affectionately called her, he had already tried to take his own life prior to his arrest at Finlow Farm.

The recommendation of mercy was denied and on Tuesday 16th November 1926 James Leah, who had spent the intervening period between sentence and execution being nursed back to health in the prison hospital, was hanged at Walton Gaol by Thomas Pierrepoint. Maybe the only mercy afforded James Leah was, as recorded by Colonel Rich, the prison governor, that Mr Pierrepoint carried out the execution 'skilfully, humanely and decorously'.

10

DEATH
OF THE ACCUSER

The Murder of Mrs Hannah White at Chester
April 1928

Hannah White never got over the death of her nephew, lost in a fishing-boat accident on the River Dee in November 1927. The 51 year old fisherman's wife had a fondness for drink and whenever she indulged, she usually let it be known, to whoever was listening, whom she blamed for her nephew's tragic death.

Living a few doors away from Mrs White, in Greenway Street, Handbridge, Chester, was 29 year old William Dobson, a respectable married man with two young children. Dobson had been in charge of the boat that fateful day on the River Dee and despite no official blame being levelled at him, it was he whom Mrs White deemed responsible for the tragedy.

On Saturday night, 7th April 1928, William Dobson returned home after a long, hard day on the river. Exhausted and ready for bed, Dobson had just entered his front door when he heard from a neighbour that he was being bad-mouthed by a drunken Mrs White. 'That's the last straw,' he told his wife, pulling on his coat and closing the door behind him. He stormed down the street in a rage and knocked upon the door at number 35, the home of Mrs White.

What happened next formed the basis of a murder trial heard before Mr Justice Shearman at Chester Assizes on 21st June, when William Dobson stood charged with the wilful murder of Mrs White.

Lord Halsbury led for the prosecution and outlined the facts as they were known. Mrs White, he said, was given to intemperance. She had, wrongly, alleged that Dobson was responsible for the death of her nephew, who died while net-fishing on the River Dee.

Greenway Street, Handbridge, Chester.

When Dobson returned home at 10 pm on 7th April he learned that she had been charging him with the tragedy; then witnesses heard him remark as he left the house that he would quieten her down.

Although no one actually witnessed Dobson strike any blows, neighbours heard an exchange of words followed shortly by the sound of screaming. As a number of neighbours came out of their homes onto the street, Dobson was seen walking away from where Mrs White lay in a heap. He was carrying a hammer and uttered casually: 'She will shout about me no more!'

Mrs White was found lying in a gutter with a terrible wound to her head. Those first to the scene could not get close to the stricken woman as her dog stood over the body, growling fiercely. It was later coaxed away, and Mrs White was carried back inside her home, but she was found to be dead before help could arrive.

In the early hours of the following morning, Chief Inspector Griffiths called at 7 Greenway Street and spoke to Dobson with regard to the murder. He made a statement and was then arrested. Dobson's defence was to be that whilst he admitted striking the woman, he had done so with his fist after shoving her away during a quarrel. 'The accusations she made preyed on my mind,' he told the court.

Contesting that the woman had died as a result of being punched,

The River Dee at Handbridge c.1920, where Dobson earned his living.

Lord Halsbury called Home Office pathologist Dr Walter Grace to the stand. Dr Grace produced in court the dead woman's skull and indicated a hole which could only have been produced by a weapon such as the hammer exhibited in court, which had been removed from a cupboard in Dobson's house.

At the suggestion of the prosecution, Dr Grace explained that such a blow would probably have been struck with the victim's head resting against something hard, such as the pavement, and he pointed out that the fracture and subsequent hole in the skull matched the shape of the hammer head perfectly. If the blow had been struck while the victim was standing up, the head would have 'rolled' with the blow, and the fracture would not have been so exact.

Dobson's elderly mother was called to speak on his behalf by the defence, but even under the leading, helpful guidance of his counsel, she was too overcome with emotion to speak coherently. At the judge's request, Lord Halsbury declined to cross-examine this witness and a similar tearful scene occurred when Dobson's sister was called to give evidence. On reaching the dock, this witness collapsed before she could take the oath and had to be carried from the court.

Concluding the defence, Dobson's counsel pleaded that he was of previous unblemished reputation, and had earned the esteem and respect of all who knew him; he had acted out of character on the greatest possible provocation.

Summing up, Mr Justice Shearman agreed with the prosecution's claim that while Dobson may have acted under the greatest provocation, it did not excuse murder. He pointed to the defence's claim that Dobson struck the fateful blow with his fist, and asked them to consider the evidence of Dr Grace when they retired to ponder a verdict.

Regardless of the rights and wrongs of Mrs White's accusations and Dobson's loss of temper, the facts before the jury were simple, and it was no surprise that they needed just a short time to return the only possible verdict on the evidence as presented. Dobson was guilty as charged. They did, however, offer a strong recommendation for mercy, which Mr Justice Shearman, after passing the sentence of death, said he would forward to the appropriate authority. Many women in the packed gallery sobbed loudly as Dobson was led from the dock.

Fortunately for Dobson, the recommendation for mercy received a sympathetic hearing and a week before his scheduled execution, word was received that he had been spared the hangman's rope. He served seven years for the murder and in August 1935 he was released from gaol to set about rebuilding his life.

11

THE
LOVERS' LANE MURDER

The Murder of Moreen Branagan at Neston
December 1945

Early on Wednesday morning, 19th December 1945, Geoffrey Groundsell was out on his usual morning stroll close to his home at Earle Crescent, Neston. His customary pre-breakfast walk took him along Wood Lane, known locally as 'Lovers' Lane', a popular spot for courting couples. He was passing the dwelling house 'Roseacre' when through the morning mist he made out the shape of something lying at the side of the road. Groundsell's first thoughts were that it was a discarded Guy from 5th November, but he nevertheless hurried home to fetch a torch.

He met up with a neighbour and the two headed back to Wood Lane where under torchlight they saw the body of a woman. From the state of her face and clothing it was clear that she had been the victim of an attack of some sort. Careful not to touch anything, the horrified men ran to fetch the police.

A cordon was quickly put around the area and a murder investigation set up, under the command of Superintendent Platt of Cheshire CID. Police inquiries soon established that the victim was 31 year old Moreen Branagan, who was employed as a barmaid at the Holywell Hotel, Parkgate, Neston, and who for the last three weeks had lodged locally with Hilda Roberts.

Hilda had been friends with Moreen for many years and it was she who had the sad duty of formally identifying the body. She was also able to help police form a picture of Moreen's lifestyle and acquaintances.

On the previous day the two women had left home together. Hilda was going to Hinderton and as they parted company, she assumed that

Wood Lane, Neston, known to locals as 'Lovers' Lane'.

Moreen was off to work as usual. Moreen had not in fact gone into work and returned home at 6 pm after a day's shopping in Liverpool. She had gone out again after tea but didn't say where she was going. Hilda thought she was going to see her fiancé, Arthur Gatenby, who lodged close by. They were both excited and eager about their forthcoming marriage, and Hilda presumed they would spend the evening discussing their future plans. She waited up for Moreen until 11.30 pm, then retired to bed.

Hilda awoke at 2.15 am, and discovered that Moreen had still not returned home. She was not unduly worried, as Moreen occasionally stayed overnight with friends.

Moreen's mother confirmed that she had last seen her daughter alive on Monday 17th December, at 4.30 pm. She also said that Moreen was physically weak, having been plagued with chest and lung problems throughout her life.

Further inquiries established that Moreen had been seen with a man on the bus from Parkgate to Neston at 8 pm on Tuesday 18th. Regulars at the Brewers Arms public house confirmed that Moreen was drinking in the pub until closing time, with a man in naval uniform. They had quite a lot to drink – 'port and beer chasers', recalled one witness – and left the pub at closing time slightly the worse for drink.

Enquiries turned to HMS *Mersey*, a local naval barracks, where it was established that James Palmer, a Glaswegian, had been demobbed on Tuesday 18th December, having served his time as a ship's steward. He was handsomely paid on his release, and three of his friends had accompanied him to a pub in Parkgate, where he stood them several rounds of drinks. He excused himself at 7.30 pm, saying he had 'a date with a girl'.

Superintendent Platt traced Palmer to Glasgow and immediately noticed scratches on his forehead, wrists and hands. He explained these away as having been caused by a cap which fitted too tightly, and a 'wee hammer used when breaking coal'! Platt examined the cap and found nothing about it which could have caused the abrasions, and was not convinced by Palmer's story.

He cautioned Palmer, who denied any knowledge of Moreen after they had left the Brewers Arms. Palmer was searched, and police found red fibres which proved a match for the mackintosh worn by Moreen on the night of her death. They also found a wristwatch with the glass face broken and the hour hand missing. The watch was the same size as a circular impression on the back of Moreen's red coat, and broken glass found at the scene was established as being from a watch face.

Palmer's naval uniform had traces of soil which matched the earth at Wood Lane, and the missing hour hand was found embedded in the sleeve. On Boxing Day 1945, satisfied of Palmer's guilt, Superintendent Platt charged him with the murder of Moreen Branagan.

The trial began on Thursday 8th February 1946 at Cheshire Assizes, before Mr Justice Stable. Opening the case for the prosecution, Mr Glyn Jones KC called Police Sergeant Easton, stationed at Neston, who had been the first to the scene. He told the court that the body had been lying on the ground, fully clothed, with legs outstretched and hair ruffled. The earth was disturbed, which indicated signs of a struggle.

After Moreen's mother had given evidence, pathologist Dr Walter Grace, who had conducted the autopsy, was next to be called. 'The woman was dead, lying on her back, slightly inclined to the right side. The exposed parts of the body, such as the arms and legs, were cold, but the unexposed parts were still warm. There was some dried blood around the mouth; and the fronts of the legs, from the knees to ankles, were spattered with mud. She was a frail woman, 5 feet 2 inches tall, and weighing just six and a half stone. I concluded she had been dead for some 12 hours.'

Continuing, Dr Grace said that there were 15 abrasions around the

The Brewers Arms, Neston.

mouth and nose area, 'linear in type, the longest being approximately three quarters of an inch long. These could have been caused by fingernails. There was a small bruise on the inside of her upper left lip, a bruise on the tip of her tongue, and a large bruise on her forehead above the left eye.'

'These injuries', Dr Grace went on, 'had been manually produced, most likely by a fist. They do not seem to have been caused by a fall, or a hard object like a wall, as in that case the skin on the forehead bruise would have been broken. These injuries combined to cause a rapid asphyxial death.' Concluding his evidence, Dr Grace said that although the deceased was frail she had put up considerable resistance, and that traces of human skin were found under her fingernails. 'Death was due to suffocating and bruising of the thyroid gland, manually produced.'

Challenged by Mr Francis Williams, leading for the defence, Dr Grace admitted that this was not an example of a particularly violent strangulation by hand. Further questioning by the defence allowed Dr Grace to reiterate Moreen's medical history, originally revealed by her mother. He agreed that Moreen was a frail, pigeon-chested woman, already suffering from chronic pleurisy, and had a breathing handicap. Dr Grace agreed with Mr Williams that any marked exertion would put added strain on her heart.

In a further reply to Mr Williams, Dr Grace said that in the woman's condition, her thyroid gland would be susceptible to shock, and agreed that in particular circumstances, the blow might have been slight.

The trial went into a second day and began with the prisoner being called to give evidence. He gave his name as James Palmer, a 33 year old merchant seaman of Walter Street, Glasgow. Asked by the defence, Palmer told of his meeting with the deceased:

'We met on a bus from Hamilton Square, Birkenhead, to Neston on 17th December, and arranged to meet on the following day. I had a drink with some friends in a pub in Parkgate, and left them to meet up with Miss Branagan. We spent the evening in the Brewers Arms drinking "ports and bitters" until closing time. I just remember leaving the public house, then the next thing I remember was Moreen standing in front of me, opposite a wall. We were kissing and this seemed to rouse me. We fell in the roadway. I fell on top of her and intimacy took place. She slapped my face and said "You shouldn't have done that", and started squirming on the ground and screaming.

'She was throwing her hands about in a claw-like manner, and I tried to catch hold of them. I did not know I had struck her at all. She seemed to go limp and her struggles ceased. I lifted her up and the next thing I remember is putting her down. I think I put her down but I'm not very sure. I got all excited and lost my head. I was looking around and saw her bag and put it beside her. I became very excited and lost my head. I went away. I turned around and just came back.'

Palmer was clearly distressed as he finished his evidence. Asked by Mr Justice Stable if he had walked past the spot where he had left the woman, he replied: 'No, sir, I just walked in the opposite direction.'

The trial finished later that afternoon with the judge summing up the main points of the evidence. Although much of the evidence was circumstantial, it was clear, from Palmer's own testimony, that he was responsible for the woman's death. It was left to the jury to decide whether they thought the prisoner was guilty of manslaughter; guilty of murder; or not guilty of murder.

Returning after deliberating for one and three-quarter hours, the foreman of the jury announced that they found Palmer guilty of murder, but added a recommendation for mercy. The judge said he felt they had returned the only verdict possible on the evidence heard in court, and proceeded to sentence Palmer to death.

Palmer was housed in the death cell at Walton Prison while efforts to support an appeal were made on his behalf. On 11th March, Palmer was escorted to the Central Criminal Court where the appeal was heard before Lord Chief Justice Goddard and two other judges. They heard the evidence as it was put at the trial and after a short recess announced that they concurred with the original finding; the appeal was dismissed.

An execution date was set for Tuesday 26th March 1946, but just three days before he was to be hanged, Palmer received word that the sentence had been commuted to life imprisonment. He served just nine years for the cruel rape and murder of a weak and unfortunate woman and on 3rd February 1955, James Palmer walked from gaol a free man.

12

FOR
THREE NIGHTS OF PASSION

The Murder of Bernard Phillips at Winsford
January 1946

The engine cut out and slowly the black Ford Eight coasted to a halt. Yet despite the darkness it did not go unnoticed. From his vantage point in a field beside Moulton Hall Farm, Winsford, the farmer watched the man shiftily look around, then briskly walk up the dirt track and disappear. It was Thursday evening, 3rd January 1946.

Making his way to work on the following morning, the farmer noticed that the car was still there. He reported it to the local police and Constable Beasley was sent to investigate. He noted the registration number, DNC 977, saw there were some eggs on the back seat, and taking a look around the immediate area, spotted a loose-leaf pocket book.

The vehicle was registered to the Refuge Lending Society and was the company car of the managing clerk of the Manchester branch, 37 year old Bernard Phillips, whose wife Kitty had reported him missing when he had failed to return to their home at 33 Meadhill Road, Prestwich, Manchester, on the previous evening.

The whereabouts of the missing clerk were discovered on Saturday afternoon. It was approaching teatime and two young brothers were making their way back to their home in Winsford. Fred and Donald Threadgold usually took the footpath that ran beside the Liverpool to Crewe railway line, but they knew that by crossing the snow-covered field next to Smokehall bridge they would complete the journey in half the time.

Climbing over a fence, they scurried up the embankment and approached the bridge. Fred was racing ahead when he noticed something unusual in the adjacent culvert. Gingerly, the brothers edged down the incline until they could clearly make out what had attracted their attention. Partly hidden in the undergrowth was the body of a man. Police quickly identified the body as that of Bernard Phillips.

At the murder scene, Home Office pathologist Dr Walter Grace quickly ascertained that the victim had been stabbed to death; when he later carried out a post-mortem he was able to say that Phillips had died from a stab wound to the left shoulder which had punctured his lung. He estimated that the victim had been dead for approximately 48 hours.

Detectives searching the culvert immediately found a vital clue when the murder weapon was recovered from beside the body. A commando bayonet, it was traced to one Harold Berry, a 30 year old father of four who worked as a watchman at Winsford's CWS bacon factory. Detectives called at his house and found that he was not at home; his wife suggested to the officers that he might be in London with a soldier's wife with whom he had been having an affair.

Several of Berry's friends and workmates were questioned and police were led by them to believe that Berry had planned to visit a friend at Pendleton, Salford, and was due back on Monday. A round-the-clock watch was kept on the house.

Tracing the events that led to the death of Bernard Phillips led police back to the previous autumn, when Harold Berry had first met 21 year old Irene Wynne, the pretty wife of a soldier serving overseas. Irene also worked at the bacon factory and the two had met when the firm arranged a works outing to Manchester's Belle Vue to celebrate the first peacetime Christmas for six years. After the outing the couple saw each other again on the next day, and during the following month they met for up to three nights a week, often drinking in the pubs and clubs around Northwich.

With her husband serving overseas, Irene had returned to live with her mother, and as Berry had a wife and four children at home, this meant that their courting was limited to furtive kissing in bus shelters and on park benches. Frustrated at being unable to take Irene to bed, Berry decided to plan a romantic weekend in London's West End. He asked Irene to accompany him and she agreed at once.

Pleased as he was with this acceptance, it now presented Berry with a problem. His meagre wages from the bacon factory were barely enough to support his wife and family, let alone pay for three nights of passion in the West End. He needed money to finance his romance, and after much deliberation he thought of a solution.

Detectives learned that at 11 am on 3rd January, Berry had called into offices of the Refuge Lending Society in Market Street, Manchester, seeking a loan of £50. Asked to fill in a number of forms, he signed them as George Wood, poultry farmer, of Moss Side Road Farm, Tarporley, Cheshire. The manager, Bernard Phillips, told the customer that because of the size of the loan he would have to visit the address in person to verify the claim before he could authorise the release of the loan. Phillips told him he would arrange to call on Sunday afternoon, as 'it would be a nice drive out for me and the wife'.

This didn't suit 'Mr Wood's' plans at all. The loan, he stressed, was urgent. After consulting his diary, the manager told him to come back that afternoon and they could sort it out then. Shortly after 2 pm, Berry and the manager, with a suitcase containing the money, set out in the black Ford Eight.

Irene Wynne had meanwhile told her mother she was going to spend the weekend with a friend, and had taken a suitcase to work with her. Berry subsequently arrived at the factory and waited for Irene to finish her shift. They called into a local public house and after a drink they were given a lift to Sale where they caught a bus into Manchester, spending the night with a friend before catching the morning train to London.

The couple caught the Monday afternoon express back to Manchester and at 7 pm, Superintendent Platt of Cheshire CID, in charge of the murder inquiry, received word that Berry had entered a house in Seedley Road, Pendleton. Accompanied by a sergeant, Superintendent Platt went to the address and questioned Berry. Asked to empty his pockets, Berry produced a wallet and cigarette lighter, found to be the property of Bernard Phillips. He was placed under arrest and taken to Northwich police station where later that night he was charged with murder.

Less than a month after the murder, Berry found himself before Mr Justice Stable at Cheshire Assizes. Mr Glyn Jones KC and Mr Arthian Davies led for the prosecution, while Berry's defence was handled by Mr Edmund Davies KC and Mr Basil Miles. He pleaded not guilty to the charge.

The first witness for the prosecution was Charles Bratt of Winsford, who testified that shortly before Christmas 1945, he sold Berry a commando knife for 10 shillings. The knife, recovered from beside the body and firmly established as the murder weapon, was held up in court.

A witness who knew Berry well told the court how he had seen him catching a Manchester-bound bus on Thursday 3rd January, and Annie Jarmaine, a cashier at the Refuge Lending Society, identified Berry as the man who had signed the paperwork as George Wood, and who had left the office in the company of Mr Phillips.

Cross-examined by Mr Edmund Davies, Miss Jarmaine admitted that she had initially told the police that the man who left with Mr Phillips had fair hair. Berry was asked to stand up in court and it was clear that his dark hair could in no way be said to be fair. The defence also managed to discredit this witness further by saying that although she would now say the man in the dock was the man who left with the manager that afternoon, she had failed to pick him out of an identity parade on the day after his arrest.

Berry was identified by several witnesses from London to whom he had given money, money since found to have been issued to Bernard Phillips on the day he disappeared. In accordance with procedures at the time, Berry had even signed his name on the back of each of the notes.

The court also heard that at 3.30 on the afternoon of 3rd January, Berry had turned up at the CWS poultry farm at Rhoden, Wellington, Shropshire, in a motor car. He asked one of the workers, Frank Dutton, a man he had known for several years, if he could spare some eggs for his children. The friend gave him half a dozen and Berry left soon after. It was alleged that these were the eggs found in the abandoned car.

Evidence was read out from Mrs Kitty Phillips, the money-lender's widow, who was too ill to attend court. At the earlier remand hearing she had been asked if she recognised a wallet found in Berry's possession. After identifying it as belonging to her husband, Mrs Phillips had turned to look at Berry and cried: 'You murderer! You murdered my husband!' In tears, she had had to be escorted back to her seat.

There was great excitement when Irene Wynne was called to the stand. She told the court of the trip to London and how Berry had showered her with expensive gifts and extravagant luxuries. She told how they had stayed in rooms costing £1 per night, when Berry's income was barely £5 a week; bought theatre tickets costing 17 shillings and 6 pence each; bought two books costing 20 shillings; and purchased tickets to the cinema and drinks in the hotel bar and other public houses. All told, Berry had spent over £20 in London.

The prosecution's evidence took up two days of the trial and on the third day the defence opened their case by calling Berry to the stand. Dressed in a neat pinstripe suit and with his black hair smartly swept back, Berry was asked by Mr Edmund Davies: 'Did you kill Bernard Phillips?'

'No, my Lord. I had never seen Mr Phillips before, nor have I visited the Refuge Lending Society offices.'

Berry was asked about his service in the Merchant Navy and he told how he had met a man named Greenwood whilst in Australia shortly before the War. Several years later he met Greenwood again in London and lent him £15.

Berry then said he had last seen Greenwood in Manchester on Wednesday 2nd January 1946, when he reminded him that he still owed some money. Greenwood told Berry if he met him in Manchester on the following day he would repay the loan. They had arranged to meet in the morning, and after meeting his friend, Berry returned home shortly after noon. At this time the debt had not been repaid, but Berry was asked to meet up with Greenwood later that afternoon, when he would receive his money.

Berry said that he had met up with Greenwood that afternoon as arranged and at Greenwood's suggestion they drove towards Whitchurch, where Berry collected the eggs. Berry said that Greenwood didn't have a key for the car and apparently started it with a 'home-made' one which looked like a screwdriver.

When Berry had met up with Greenwood that afternoon, Berry wasn't short of money. He said that he had collected some £11 from a tontine club, sold some poultry for a similar amount, and received £17 from a winning transaction with an illegal corner bookmaker. Greenwood then paid back the loan, adding an extra £5 of 'interest' for the delay. He peeled off two £5 notes and ten £1 notes from two wallets. Berry asked if Greenwood could spare a wallet and he was given the one produced in court. Greenwood also gave Berry a lighter; this too was produced as evidence.

Berry said that the dagger purchased from Charlie Bratt was sold in a Northwich public house that same night. Mrs Berry had told her husband to get rid of it after finding one of the children playing with it, and Berry said he sold it to a soldier in a pub for 25 shillings. He couldn't remember which public house it had been, nor the name of the soldier, but he had seen him regularly in the town.

In closing their summing-up, the prosecution counsel, who had called a total of 40 witnesses, suggested that Berry's whole story was pure fabrication and could not be substantiated by any facts.

Summing up for the defence, Mr Edmund Davies said that whilst the case might be deemed a 'sordid one' because of the way Berry had acted in relation to his family, such considerations should not affect the jury's judgement when considering a verdict. He also pointed out that the only witness who had identified Berry in the company of Mr Phillips was Miss Jarmaine, whose evidence had been shown not to be satisfactory. He emphasised that Berry was not short of money, as he had shown in his evidence.

Asked to consider a verdict, the jury took less than an hour to find Berry guilty as charged, the only possible verdict on the evidence presented, and he was sentenced to death. His appeal was unsuccessful and on Tuesday morning, 9th April 1946, Harold Berry was hanged at Strangeways Prison, Manchester.

One wonders whether Berry, awaiting execution, counted the true cost of his 'dirty weekend' in London's West End. The lives of two men, the widowing of two women, and four young children left without a father: that was the true price of Harold Berry's and Irene Wynne's three nights of passion.

'Capital Punishment
Amendment Act, 1868

(31 & 32 Vict. c. 24, s. 7)

The sentence of the law passed upon   HAROLD BERRY   found guilty of murder, will be carried into execution at *9* a.m. to-morrow.

Percy Macdonald Sheriff of *Lancashire*
C. T. Cope Governor.
8th April 1946
Manchester Prison.

No. 278.

81

13

WHO KILLED
CLARA CROPPER?

The Murder of Clara Cropper at Ellesmere Port
July 1948

The grim discovery of the decompos-
ing, naked body of a middle-aged woman was made by two teenage
boys. The afternoon of Thursday 12th August 1948 was a scorcher and
the two lads were enjoying the summer sunshine by searching for scrap
metal in some long grass beside the old cement works offices at
Pontoon, Ellesmere Port.

While one of the lads lifted some blackberry bushes, his friend pulled
out a rusted bicycle frame, and as he did so both were greeted by a
rotten stench that they took to be a dead dog. A closer look revealed
something far more sinister. Thirteen year old John Burne, who along
with his friend, 14 year old William Gorman, had made the gruesome
discovery, rushed home to tell his parents, and they in turn sent him to
tell the police.

Officers hurried to the scene and after the area was cordoned off,
they searched the surrounding land with scythes in the hope of finding
clues to the identity of the woman, a task that seemed to be hampered
by the absence of clothing and advanced state of decomposition.

Police suspected from the outset that the body was that of 41 year old
Mrs Clara Cropper, who had been reported missing from her home at
Lees Cottage, Cromwell Road, Pontoon, on 2nd July. The theory
seemed correct when several items of women's clothing, retrieved from
the nearby Shropshire Union canal, were identified as belonging to the
missing woman, but it was to be two weeks later before a positive
identification was established when a set of dentures found among
bushes on the wasteland were confirmed as those of Mrs Cropper.

Home Office pathologist Dr Walter Grace reported that death

seemed to have been caused by blows to the right side of the face and jaw, possibly by a bottle. Two empty but unbroken beer bottles found beside the body appeared to support this.

Investigations into the last known movements of the missing woman suggested that she had been in the company of a Norwegian sailor whose ship SS *Borgholn* had been berthed at Bowater's Wharf.

Police learned that on the night of 2nd July, Arthur Hindle was returning home from a dance at the Majestic Ballroom when he saw a woman lying on the grass close to where the body was later found. A man was standing nearby, and as the witness thought that they were a courting couple, he passed by quickly without a word. His evidence was later to play a crucial part in the trial.

The Norwegian sailor was 53 year old Olaf Andrea Flaathe, whom police had interviewed two days after Mrs Cropper had been reported missing. Flaathe admitted being with Mrs Cropper on the Friday night (2nd July). 'I left her at Edie Gill's house. She was in a hurry to catch a bus, but did not tell me where she was going.' Flaathe then made a written statement and added at its conclusion: 'I hope you find her, it looks bad for me.'

Things did indeed look bad for the sailor when on 26th August, Detective Inspector Welsh and Detective Sergeant Meakin, in charge of the investigation, travelled down to Gravesend, Kent, and arrested Flaathe on board his ship, now moored on the River Thames. Flaathe was again questioned and this time placed under arrest. 'I am not guilty of this charge', he protested as he was led away.

Olaf Flaathe was tried for the murder of Clara Cropper before Mr Justice Pritchard at Chester Assizes in November. Mr Arthian Davies KC opened for the Crown and outlined the case for the prosecution. He told the packed court that on the night of Friday 2nd July, the prisoner joined Mrs Cropper and her friend Mrs Edith Gill in the Canal Tavern public house, Pontoon. At closing time the three returned to Mrs Gill's house at 7 Sunnyside. Flaathe and Mrs Cropper then left the house together and she was never seen alive again. At this time Flaathe was a seaman employed on a vessel moored at Bowater's Wharf, Ellesmere Port.

On 12th August, the naked body of a woman was discovered lying in thick grass about 130 yards from the back door of no 7 Sunnyside. The face had been 'bashed in'; Mr Davies asserted that she had been murdered and that the man in the dock had murdered her.

Continuing with his opening address, Davies told the jury that there

Clara Cropper.

were three questions facing them:
1. Was the body that of Mrs Cropper?
2. Was she murdered?
3. Was it the prisoner who murdered her?

The Crown called to the stand Sergeant Axton, who had been among the first to the scene after the body was discovered. Sergeant Axton produced a plan of the area and indicated where he and fellow officers had searched for clues and where they had found the empty beer bottles, neither of which bore labels. He also indicated where items of clothing had been fished from the Shropshire canal; after a number of experiments it had been concluded the clothing had drifted from the north, suggesting that it had been deposited in the water just beside the Colas bridge, close to where the body was found.

Pathologist Dr Walter Grace told the court that the post-mortem he had carried out found that the appearance of the body was consistent with death occurring on or about 2nd July 1948. He also stated that the woman's injuries were consistent with her having met a violent end and that death was due to intracranial haemorrhage resulting from the multiple fractures of the bones of the face.

In answer to a question by Mr Justice Pritchard, Dr Grace said that these injuries could well have been caused by a beer bottle, as in order for a bottle to break on impact, it would have to strike a hard, resistant surface. The human face, comprised of soft flesh and tissue, would yield to the blow and not cause enough resistance to cause the bottle to break.

Next to the stand was Richard Bell, who had lived with Clara Cropper since 1940. He had identified the dentures found beside the body as belonging to Clara.

Bell was followed into the witness box by Clara Cropper's daughter Georgina, who told the court that she saw her mother leaving the Canal Tavern with Mrs Gill and the prisoner on 2nd July. On the following night she saw her grandmother, Mrs Smith, ask Flaathe where he had left Clara on the previous night, and if he had given her money. She said that the accused said he had given her no money and that she had left him to catch a bus to Hull.

Adeline Cropper, another daughter of the deceased, told the court that on Sunday 4th July, Flaathe had spoken to her in the Canal Tavern and asked if she had seen her mother. She replied in the negative, so Flaathe asked if she would pass on a message and wrote down his name and address on a piece of paper. This was later pointed out by the judge as a key point in the defence.

The main witness for the Crown was to be Arthur Hindle, who had seen a man on the footpath as he came home from a dance. Asked by the prosecuting counsel if he recognised that man in court, Hindle said: 'Yes. It is the man in the dock.'

'Have you any doubts about that?' he was asked.

'No, I don't think so.'

This key witness was cross-examined by Mr Edmund Davies, leading for the defence. 'Have you entertained any doubts about the man in the dock?' he asked.

'I did at first,' Hindle replied.

Flaathe's counsel scored an impressive victory with this witness when they got him to admit that it was a dark, moonless night and he hadn't stopped on the footpath long enough to get a good look at the man.

Summing up at the end of the trial, Mr Justice Pritchard said that the case hinged on the evidence of Arthur Hindle, and he asked them to consider it seriously. He also asked the jury if it was conceivable that a man should return to the Canal Tavern and leave a message for Clara Cropper if he knew she was already dead. Mr Justice Pritchard said that he wondered why he and the jury had not seen Mrs Smith. In her absence, the jury had to consider what other people said they had heard her say to the accused.

The jury took just eight minutes to acquit the prisoner. Cheers rang out as he shook hands with his Norwegian interpreter and walked from the dock a free man.

As Flaathe left the country, serving on board a new ship, one important question remained unanswered: 'Who killed Clara Cropper?' Nearly 50 years later, the identity of her killer is still a mystery.

14

'MUM'S
THE WORD!'

The Murder of Pearl Cowman at Stalybridge
August 1949

Despite the late hour and a fear of the dark, at 10.15 pm, on Wednesday 24th August 1949, 13 year old Pearl Cowman called at the chip shop to buy supper for herself and her grandmother. With a half-crown in her gymslip, she had skipped along Stalybridge High Street, away from the Oddfellows' Club where she had accompanied her grandmother and two uncles as a treat. She never returned with the supper.

During the night and on the following days an intensive search was made of the surrounding area. Mrs Evelyn Tansey, whose house overlooked the Huddersfield canal, told police that twice during that Wednesday night she heard a girl's voice from the canal bank. Firstly, at 11.15 pm, she heard what sounded like a young girl talking, and about two hours later she was awoken by a muffled shout.

'I couldn't be sure what she was saying,' she told police. 'It sounded like "David", but it could have been "Save me". I looked out of my window, but it was pitch dark and I could not see or hear anything, so I went back to bed.'

Police concentrated the search in the area around Caroline Street, Stanley Square and the surrounding streets, but it was over 36 hours later, at 10.30 am on Friday, when four young boys discovered Pearl Cowman's body floating in the Huddersfield canal.

At first sight Pearl was fully clothed and apparently uninjured, and it seemed that she might have been the victim of a tragic accident, but once the results of the post-mortem came through it became clear that police had a murder inquiry on their hands. The spot where Pearl was found in the water would have necessitated a detour of some 400 yards, and as the youngster was afraid of the dark, it seemed clear that she had been lured to the bank, rather than chanced upon it.

As the investigation was stepped up, police learned that Pearl had been seen in the company of a man at 10.30 on that Wednesday night. Schoolgirl Lucy Bennett told police she had seen Pearl skipping down the street, watched from the entrance of a public house by a man of whom she was able to give a good description. 'He was following her with his eyes,' she told detectives.

On Thursday 1st September, with the investigation still the centre of attention amongst the locals, inside a Stalybridge cotton mill a strange conversation took place between two workers. Cotton worker Alice Roberts was at her machine discussing the murder when she was interrupted by 41 year old Henry Taylor. 'The police and the people rule the world, the organ player will send me to the gallows!' he declared.

Stunned by this strange outburst, Alice spoke to Taylor later that morning, and asked him what he meant. Sweating profusely, his hair wet with perspiration, Taylor said: 'I smell of death. I've smelt of death all week.' He then told her he had intended throwing himself under a bus and had gone to the mill window three times to throw himself out, but each time his nerve failed him. 'They say they've got someone named Walton, but Henry Taylor did it.'

Alice asked him if he had killed the young girl on the canal bank. 'Yes, but mum's the word. One word from you will put a rope around my neck.' Alice told him that if he knew anything about the murder it would be in his best interests to tell the police, and he said that he would. True to his word, later that afternoon, as two detectives passed his house carrying out other inquiries, Taylor called them over.

'I want to tell you something about the girl,' he told Detective Sergeant Mitchell. Cautioned, Taylor made a statement, after the officer allegedly told him: 'You had better tell me the truth. I always find out, even if I have to go to the ends of the world. I will be a friend to you if you tell me the truth.'

When Henry Taylor stood before Mr Justice Hallett on 7th November 1949, at Chester Assizes, the prosecution had a formidable case against him. The schoolgirl witness testified to seeing Taylor watch Pearl skipping down High Street, while another witness told how he had seen a man later identified as Taylor leading a young girl towards the canal.

Mr Vincent Lloyd Jones KC said that Taylor had committed a dreadful

The Huddersfield canal at Stalybridge.

murder. He told the court that whilst drunk the accused had lured Pearl, whom he knew, to the canal bank where he tried to sexually assault her. He then pulled out a knife and cut at her clothes. Mr Jones then said that Taylor, fearful that Pearl would report him for the attempted assault, panicked and threw her into the murky water. Four times she crawled to the bank and four times he threw her back in, watching her drown as her strength slowly sapped away.

Faced with a strong case, Mr F Elwyn Jones KC, leading for the defence, suggested that whilst Taylor might well have been on the canal bank as suggested, the actual cause of death was very different from that which the Crown had alleged. Taylor, he said, had made an attempted assault, which Pearl had fought off, and while trying to flee she had fallen into the canal. Taylor, Mr Jones went on, tried to pull her from the water, but being unable to swim, he was forced to watch helplessly as the water dragged her down.

Summing up, the judge told the jury that the case hinged on how they believed Pearl Cowman met her death. The jury of ten men and two women needed just a short time to return a guilty verdict.

'It isn't true!' Taylor shouted from the dock, when asked if he had anything to say before sentence was passed.

'You have rightly been convicted of a cruel murder for which only one sentence is known to our law,' Mr Justice Hallett told the prisoner as he sentenced him to be hanged.

Taylor announced that he wished to appeal and on Monday 12th December Lord Chief Justice Goddard headed a panel of judges appointed to decide Taylor's fate. After a recount of the key points of the trial, Lord Goddard announced that Taylor had committed a 'wholly shocking and terrible murder' and there were no grounds for interfering with the verdict.

Little sympathy was shown for the fate of Taylor, who was returned to the death cell at Strangeways Prison, Manchester; the residents of Stalybridge were still shocked at the dreadful tragedy. Mercy was, however, shown to the unworthy killer, when less than 48 hours before he was to die, it was announced that Henry Taylor would not hang; instead, he was sentenced to life imprisonment.

15

A DECADE
OF DERISION

The Murder of Norah Cobon at Altrincham
September 1951

Frederick George Cobon was born in
Altrincham in 1912. He was raised from infancy by his aunt, Mrs Emily
Alice Hudson, and she was the lady he knew as 'mother'. Cobon
prospered as a young man, becoming director of the family company,
Watson and Hudson Ltd, and enjoyed a happy life with his wife and
two young children.

All seemed well until tragedy struck in 1940, when his wife died and
at 28 years old, Fred Cobon found himself widowed with two
youngsters. Aunt Alice helped him cope but he missed the love of a
wife. Fortune seemed to smile on him again, though, when he met and
married his second wife, Norah. She was a passionate if volatile woman
and their union soon produced a daughter, Catherine, on whom Fred
Cobon doted.

However, despite the blessing of a child of their own, and assistance
from the obliging Aunt Alice, who lived with them at Grey Road,
Altrincham, Norah Cobon soon dropped the genteel façade which had
attracted Frederick to her, and gave vent to displays of unprovoked
temper and spiteful nastiness, some of it directed at Aunt Alice.

Not only out of love and gratitude because she had raised him from a
child, but also because she was a majority shareholder in the company
where he worked, Fred Cobon was loath to criticise his aunt; to avoid
constant arguments with his spouse, he opted for the 'quiet life' and did
not respond to Norah's outbursts.

Unable to provoke a response from her husband, Norah would often
strike him, and as she was a very powerful woman, these assaults were
more than just petulant slaps. Frederick Cobon worried secretly about

91

his health. He had developed an acute pain in his right ribs and his fears were exacerbated when during one outburst, his wife scoffed at him: 'No doubt you have cancer!'

Civility and intimacy dwindled between them and upon the arrival of their third child in April 1948, Norah declared that she would have no further marital relations with him until he agreed to be sterilised. In the May of that year Cobon consulted Dr Barnet Gold, the family doctor, to arrange for sterilisation, more commonly referred to these days as a vasectomy. In these more enlightened times, many men see a vasectomy as a practical solution to a burgeoning family, but back in the late 1940s, for a man of 36 even to consider such an operation was considered a tragic sacrifice of his manhood. Devoted, or maybe henpecked, husband that he was, Fred Cobon persisted with his request and was finally sterilised in November 1948, at a private nursing home in Manchester.

Having agreed without demur to his wife's request, Fred Cobon hoped that relations would resume between them, but Norah remained cold and unresponsive to him. It rankled within him that he had been cheated of his manhood, and had no choice but to continue in a marriage which provided rows on an almost daily basis, but none of the joys of 'making up' afterwards.

On 4th September 1951, when Fred Cobon returned home from work, his wife insisted that he took her out as she was bored. They went to the cinema and on their return she went to bed. Having no reason to rush up and join her, Fred sat downstairs for a while and was soon joined by his aunt who had come down for a chat.

When Fred finally retired, his wife hurled a torrent of abuse at him regarding Aunt Alice: 'What did that old bitch want, coming downstairs to you?'

'There's no need to call her that, she just wanted a chat,' he said.

Disinclined to argue with his wife, Fred said no more and turned over to sleep. Norah woke him again in the early hours of 5th September and continued to debase him and his family. She punctuated her verbal assault with blows to his already painful ribs, until, with a final cutting remark, she turned her back on him.

Frederick Cobon had borne much adversity in his life. From abandonment by his natural mother, and the death of his first wife, to enforced vasectomy and the continual cold, callous nagging of his second wife, he had taken all this calmly, as befitted his reputation as a kind and gentle man. It was somehow, then, sadly appropriate and in character when on the following morning he walked up to the front desk at Sowerby Bridge police station, Yorkshire, and announced calmly and without drama: 'I have killed my wife in Altrincham.'

Police arrived shortly at 'Northlands', the Cobon family home in Grey Road, and found Norah Cobon dead in her bed. She had been shot in the back at close range, and her throat and wrists had been cut.

By his own words, Cobon was responsible for the death of his wife, but was it due to a moment of madness, or did she die as the result of a premeditated act? This was the question facing the jury at Chester Assizes on 30th October 1951, when he was charged with the wilful murder of his wife.

Defence counsel, Mr Edmund Davies KC, served his client well, calling witnesses to testify to Frederick Cobon's unhappy home life. His aunt, Mrs Emily Alice Hudson, told the court: 'Norah had a temper that was lunacy. She would throw her arms about for nothing. Frederick was very quiet and always peaceable. He avoided quarrels with his wife wherever possible.'

Dr Barnet Gold, the family doctor, testified that his patient was a kind and gentle man. 'I tried to dissuade him from sterilisation, as it is unheard of for a man of 36 to take such an irrevocable step, but he said his wife would have no more to do with him sexually until it was done. It was at her insistence that he proceeded.'

Cobon himself was called to the stand, and told the court how he had been belittled and domineered throughout his ten-year marriage. 'I took the passive course, and gave way to her all the time. She often insulted me in front of other people, and I had more peace at the office than I did at home!'

Questioned about the gun by Mr Glyn Jones KC, leading for the Crown, Cobon said that he had acquired it four years earlier and knew that there were four rounds in it. 'I did not usually keep it in the bedroom, and until 5th September I had never fired it. I usually carried it with me in the car and would not have known if the safety catch was on or off.'

Recalling the events prior to the shooting, Cobon told the court: 'She hurled abuse at me. I reached for the gun with my left hand, intending to frighten her. I brought it over and somehow she seemed to move and the gun went off. I did not intend to do her any harm whatsoever, certainly not to kill her.'

At this point, the judge, Mr Justice Hallett, intervened. Addressing Cobon, he asked: 'So the trouble you had with her had nothing to do with it? You didn't lose your temper with her?'

'No,' he replied, and went on to say that he remembered the gun going off ; his next recollection was of approaching the police station at Sowerby Bridge.

Mr Glyn Jones, however, said he was not convinced by this story and questioned why a will, dated 4th September 1951, was found in Cobon's possession. Although invalid, as it had not been properly witnessed, it divided up Cobon's property equally between his children. He had also written a letter to his aunt on that same date, but when questioned about them, Cobon stated that he was unable to remember writing any such letter or will.

Summing up what he said had been a difficult case, Mr Justice Hallett urged the jury not to be governed by their emotions, but to concern themselves with the facts:

'I thought at one time that the break-up of this man's marriage was an appeal to your emotions. The terrible incident of 1948 cannot be trivialised, but would that, after three years, cause a sudden loss of self-control? When a man has shot through the back a woman who has given him hell for ten years, what is it more likely to be: accidental or intentional?'

Thus directed, the jury duly found Frederick Cobon guilty of murder and he was sentenced to death. An appeal was heard before Lord Goddard on 28th November 1951, but was dismissed. Although usually unsympathetic in hearing murder trial appeals, Lord Goddard said that he pitied the condemned man; however, nothing had been heard at the appeal to change the due course of the law.

As the clock ticked on towards the scheduled date of Cobon's execution, word came through that mercy had been shown and the sentence of death was commuted to life imprisonment. Frederick Cobon served seven years and in October 1958 he walked out of prison a free man.

Maybe it was felt that he served his sentence before actually committing the crime, as before he made that one fateful act of retaliation, Frederick George Cobon had already endured a decade of derision.

16

DEFECT
OF REASON

The Murder of Marie Bradshaw at Crewe
February 1954

Marie and George Bradshaw were married in 1948 and lived in Alfred Street, Bury, Lancashire. Although they had two children, theirs was a turbulent union with faults on both sides, and when, shortly after New Year 1954, George found his wife in bed with a neighbour, 23 year old Milton Taylor, they had a fierce quarrel and parted for a while. They were reconciled shortly afterwards, but were unable to settle their differences; Marie eventually left George and went to live in Crewe with Milton Taylor.

They took a flat together in a house in Underwood Lane, Crewe, and for a time they seemed happy enough. On Saturday 20th February, they were visited at the flat by Marie's estranged husband George. The reason for his visit was twofold: to ask her to forget the past and return home with him, and also to be a character witness for him in a case brought against him by another woman – for an affiliation order. Adding to this confused state of events, Marie revealed to her husband that she was pregnant by Taylor. Bradshaw agreed to accept the child if they could put the past behind them and start anew.

The ensuing, sometimes heated, discussions attracted the attention of the landlady, Mrs Winifred Gregory. She had been introduced to Milton and Marie as Mr and Mrs Taylor and now, realising their true status, she told them to pack their belongings and leave.

'I do not want this flat being used for inappropriate liaisons,' she told them as they left the house in the company of George Bradshaw.

The three of them walked to Crewe Square, from where George Bradshaw returned to Bury. Milton and Marie were last seen together at around 10 pm that night in a Nantwich snack bar. With little money and

95

no bed for the night, they took shelter in a storage hut in a field, on Windy Arbour Farm, Worleston, secretly thanking the workman who had forgotten to lock it at the end of his working day.

Despite the trying circumstances, the couple had been observed as having a genuine affection for each other, but by 9 am the next day, Marie was dead, murdered by her lover.

When Milton Taylor stood trial for her murder at Chester Assizes on 5th June 1954, before Mr Justice Byrne, the story of how this apparently happy couple became murderer and victim unfolded before a packed assembly.

On Sunday morning, 21st February, Milton Taylor called on his friend, John Lee Mann, at his lodgings in an agricultural workers' hostel. Giving evidence to the court, Mann recalled:

'He came round on the Sunday morning, about 10 am. We exchanged greetings then he said, "I'm in trouble, John, I've killed Marie." I replied, "Oh aye!" thinking he was joking. He then repeated, "I've killed Marie." He was very agitated and as he came across the room to me he broke down in tears. I calmed him down and asked him why he did it. He said she'd been grumbling about stomach pains and nattering at him. I asked him if he knew what he was doing and he said: "Yes, I meant to kill her." He showed me his hands, which still had blood on them. We decided to go to the police station at Nantwich.'

The story was then continued by Sergeant Thomas Samuel Shone, of Nantwich police. He told the court how Taylor had come into the station to give himself up, as he had killed a woman. He was cautioned, then revealed: 'I did it this morning. She is in a hut in a field off the Middlewich Road. She would not let me sleep. She got on my nerves, so I strangled her with my tie and covered her face with a head-scarf. She lived with me as my wife in Crewe. I did it at about 8.40 this morning. She got on my nerves in the hut so I strangled her.' Sergeant Shone added that the accused was not wearing a neck-tie and that though his hands were dirty, there were no other marks on them.

Defending counsel, Mr Edmund Davies QC questioned the sergeant with regard to Taylor's attitude and demeanour. Shone confirmed that from his first confession, Taylor seemed very calm and collected, seemingly unaffected by the serious charge against him. He agreed with Mr Davies that Taylor's attitude throughout had been remarkable. Whilst in prison, Taylor had undergone tests which showed that he had a low mental age, but when the question of Taylor's literacy was put to the sergeant, he said he was unable to comment.

George and Marie Bradshaw on their wedding day in 1948.

Medical evidence came from Dr Hugh Blacklay of Nantwich, who had examined Marie Bradshaw's body in the hut, and from Dr Charles St Hill, the Home Office pathologist from Liverpool, who had performed the post-mortem approximately six hours after the murder was reported.

It was confirmed that death was due to asphyxia, caused by strangulation. A man's neck-tie was knotted tightly around Marie's neck, and her face was covered by a red handkerchief, ironically embroidered with the message: 'Good luck'.

With these facts established, it was plain that Milton Taylor had indeed strangled Marie Bradshaw. Although he had pleaded not guilty to the charge, Mr Davies, defending, did not challenge the irrefutable facts of the case, but made efforts to establish Taylor's state of mind. This avenue was first pursued when Sergeant Shone was questioned, and expanded upon with the evidence of further medical witnesses.

Dr Isaac Frost, consultant psychiatrist to the Liverpool Regional Hospital Board, attached to the Deva Hospital, Chester, told the court that throughout his examination of Taylor, the accused had 'smiled in a fatuous and irrelevant way', not at all appropriate for the circumstances he was in. Frost had also conducted various IQ tests with Taylor and concluded that he was feeble-minded, with the mental age of an 11 year old.

Dr Frost had questioned Taylor regarding the murder and was surprised at his reply. Taylor had said: 'I strangled somebody, sometime in February. I wanted to. Just felt like it. She didn't upset me. I got satisfaction. Just felt better when I did it with a tie. When I want to do a thing I do it, whatever the consequences. If I felt like it, I would do it to anybody else. I think anybody should strangle anybody if they feel like it. If they feel like it, it would be right from their point of view. The way I look at it, it was right to do it. I don't feel sad or sorry; quite happy as a matter of fact.'

Taylor agreed with Dr Frost that other people would think such a thing was wrong. He also said he knew it was against the law. Dr Frost added that Taylor had suffered from inflammation of the brain following a vaccination, and it was thus his opinion that Taylor was labouring under a 'defect of reason' and did not know the nature of what he was doing or that it was wrong on that February morning.

In reply, Mr F Elwyn Jones QC, leading for the Crown, called Dr F Brisby, principal medical officer at Walton Gaol, Liverpool. He testified that he had found no history of mental illness in Taylor's family, nor anything to indicate that Taylor was suffering from mental disorder or inflammation of the brain,

Also called to support the prosecution's efforts to refute the insanity charge was Dr A McKenzie, medical officer at Shrewsbury Prison, who had also had an opportunity to view Taylor whilst on remand. He too had concluded that the prisoner knew the nature of his act and that it was wrong.

The opposing counsel were well matched, but despite the copious and complex medical evidence placed before them, the jury took just 35 minutes to find Milton Taylor guilty of murder. An appeal was launched on the ground that Taylor was mentally ill, but this was rejected; the appeal judges commented that this evidence had been fully explored at the trial.

Unlike the last Taylor to be sentenced to death at Chester Assizes, (see Chapter 14) in this case there was to be no mercy shown, and on 22nd June 1954, Milton Taylor was hanged at Walton Gaol, Liverpool.

The inconsistency in the granting of reprieves during the final years of capital punishment caused a good deal of unease in the minds of many people. The execution of Milton Taylor did nothing to allay this disquiet.

17

POISONED
BY JEALOUSY

The Murder of Vivian Howard at Lymm
December 1958

Love and trust are the usual basis for a happy marriage. But while love may remain, once the trust is replaced by suspicion and jealousy, a marriage can often crumble. A sad case from the Warrington area in the late 1950s is a typical example.

Joseph and Josephine Neary were married in Ireland in 1953. Twenty-three years of age at the time of the marriage, Joseph was a conscientious and devoted husband; he served many years as an apprentice cobbler until the economic climate forced him to seek work on the British mainland.

He left his native Ireland alone in September 1954, and worked in Birmingham until June of the following year, when he was forced to return home after his wife became ill during pregnancy. Neary found temporary work until Josephine was nursed back to health, when he again left his wife and baby, and found work in England. After a visit to her husband during the spring of 1957, Josephine and the child moved over permanently later that year, by which time Neary was working in Sheffield.

A change in employment saw the Neary family relocate to Warrington later in 1957. Joseph found work at Thames Board Mills Ltd, and they took lodgings with a Mrs Talbot in Brookfield Rd, Lymm. Neary became a close friend of Michael Hughes, a fellow worker at Thames Mills, but the friendship foundered when word reached Neary that Hughes had escorted Josephine to a dance while he was working a nightshift. When challenged by her husband, she admitted this and Neary attacked Hughes with such ferocity that he was subsequently off work for two weeks.

By March 1958, relations between Neary and his wife had become strained and she left him minding the children while she sought fresh lodgings for herself elsewhere in Warrington. Coincidentally, there was a dance being held that very evening at the Dingle Ballroom, and Neary, having suspicions based on previous experience, put the children to bed early and headed for the dance hall.

Hughes's car was parked outside and on the back seat was Josephine's suitcase. Entering the dance hall, Neary saw Hughes dancing with another woman while Josephine stood by the bar. Despite his pleas, she refused to return home with him, so he flung her to the floor in a violent rage. He tried to start a fight with Hughes, but the man refused to retaliate and Neary was ejected from the dance hall.

A few weeks passed, tempers cooled, and Neary and his wife were reunited. It was a short-lived reunion and by late October, tension and unpleasantness had once again grown between them, and so they separated. The break-up was against Neary's wishes, and when he refused to move out he had to be evicted from Brookfield Road by the police. He took new lodgings with a Mrs Jackson on Ellesmere Road, Lower Walton.

Despite previous differences between them, Neary and Hughes had remained on fairly amicable terms and on Sunday 21st December, Neary visited Michael Hughes at his lodgings on Thynne Street, Warrington. The conversation eventually turned to Neary's estranged wife, and Hughes stated quite plainly that he was not seeing Josephine and really wanted nothing to do with Neary or his wife after all the past trouble.

Neary remained convinced that his wife was 'going about with another man'. Hughes was alleged to have told Neary she was involved with 'a bookie' (a statement he later denied in court), and Neary returned to his lodgings obsessed by the notion of this affair. Neary suspected that the bookie was 48 year old Vivian Aubrey Howard, who kept a shop in Lymm, and visions of Howard and Josephine together plagued him as he tossed and turned throughout the night.

Neary went to work as usual the next morning, and by lunchtime of that day, Mr Howard's fate was sealed. Neary purchased a leather-cutting knife from a shop on Market Street and cycled to Lymm. His intention was to disfigure Howard as revenge for philandering with Josephine and at the same time to pay back his wife for her adultery by letting her see her lover mutilated.

He entered the bookie's office at 16 Bridgewater Street at around

Bridgewater Street, Lymm, where bookmaker Vivian Howard had his office.

12.30 pm, and set about Howard, causing him some dozen or so wounds: eight were facial, one was in the back, another was to the back of the head, with the remainder along his left arm, which Howard had raised in self-defence.

Having taken what he considered to be fair revenge, Neary immediately went to Lymm police station and, handing the knife to the desk constable, gave himself up. He was questioned and initially charged with 'wounding with intent to murder'. Answering the charge, Neary replied: 'I did not intend to murder him, just disfigure him.'

Regardless of Neary's intent, the charge was raised to murder when later that day Vivian Howard died from his injuries – his lungs collapsed as a result of the wound to his back. At Altrincham Magistrates' Court on Tuesday 23rd December, Joseph Neary was formally charged with wilful murder and remanded in custody.

Neary's two-day trial took place at Chester Assizes on Wednesday 18th February 1959, before Mr Justice Edmund Davies. Following the Homicide Act of 1957, which categorised different types of murder, Neary was charged with the lesser non-capital murder, and all the evidence was heard on the first day. Mr Roderic Bowen QC led for the prosecution, while Mr W L Mars-Jones QC pleaded for the defence.

On the morning of the second day, Mr Justice Davies summed up the key points to the jury. The judge informed the jury that whilst Neary was clearly devoted to his wife and children, he had, by his counsel's own words, been 'poisoned by jealousy', and on this occasion, that jealousy had led him to commit murder.

Neary had expressed great remorse for the death of his victim and the sorrow of the bereaved family, and as he had, in effect, now lost his own wife and children, he stated that 'it would give him great pleasure to die.'

This may well have been a false bravado, as irrespective of his sentiment, Neary knew full well that a conviction for non-capital murder did not carry the death sentence. He seemed resigned to the verdict and showed no emotion when the jury returned to find him guilty as charged.

Sentenced to life imprisonment, Neary was escorted from the dock and led away, to reflect for the rest of his life on the consequences of his irrational and jealous behaviour.

18

MURDER
COMES TO MOULDSWORTH

The Murders of Claudine Liebert, Monique Liebert and
Daniel Berland at Mouldsworth
July 1971

At the beginning of the 1970s the tiny
village of Mouldsworth didn't even warrant a mention in the local area
guidebooks. Like many other picturesque hamlets, it was admired by
the tourists who passed through on their way to Delamere Forest. Back
in 1962, Mouldsworth had enjoyed a brief minor celebrity status with
the arrival of a nightingale in the village. People came from miles
around to hear it sing at dusk, and when the bird took flight after a few
days, Mouldsworth returned to its previous sleepy ways.

But nine years later, Mouldsworth would again find itself the centre
of attention, though this time the visitor was nothing so innocent as a
nightingale. In the summer of 1971, murder came to Mouldsworth, and
it would be a long time before the little village would find peace and
tranquillity again.

The Goshawk, Mouldsworth's only public house, enjoyed a good
trade on the sunny afternoon of Sunday 11th July 1971. Amongst those
enjoying the sunshine were many foreign tourists who flocked to the
area, often pitching their tents in the forest or staying in the local youth
hostel.

Amongst the foreign holidaymakers who took a drink at the
Goshawk later that Sunday evening were three young French tourists,
22 year old Monique Liebert, her sister Claudine, 20, and Claudine's
fiancé, Daniel Berland, also aged 20. The three had travelled from their
homes in western France and planned to tour the British countryside
during the summer holidays. As a teacher, Monique enjoyed a long
summer break, as did students Claudine and Daniel.

Mouldsworth. Less than 100 yards from this sign, three French campers were murdered.

They had arrived, like thousands of visitors each year, by the Dover ferry just five days earlier in their beige Citroën, and had headed straight for the sights of London. From there they travelled to Reading and Bristol, crossing the suspension bridge over the Avon Gorge, then on to the South Wales coast. Their adventures were meticulously recorded by Monique in her little red diary, which told of the fun they had, whether youth hostelling or camping in their small tent.

They had left Pembrokeshire after breakfast on Sunday 11th July, and were beginning to tire as they approached Cheshire; they studied their local map and debated whether to press on to Delamere Youth Hostel or to pitch their tent in the forest. After stopping for a drink at the Goshawk, they opted to give the hostel a miss and camp out close to Delamere Forest. It was a fatal decision.

That same afternoon, some forty miles away, in the village of Barlaston, near Stone in Staffordshire, another hostelry had a slightly less convivial atmosphere. The usual Sunday lunchtime attraction at the Plume of Feathers, local pianist Michael Bassett, was absent.

As well as having musical ability, 24 year old Bassett was an amateur poet and writer. Although he earned a steady wage as a book salesman, topped up by money for his piano playing, his lifestyle failed to provide either an adequate outlet for or recognition of his artistic talents. He

The Goshawk, Mouldsworth.

became depressed and dissatisfied, his mood worsening when his latest novel was rejected by several publishers. Hence his absence from the keyboard that afternoon as he took a short holiday to Rhyl, in an attempt to raise his spirits.

The lively atmosphere of the holiday resort failed to cheer him, though, and as the last of his holiday money dwindled away, so did his self-esteem. He may well have already worked out a plan to end his life when, with a reasonable knowledge of guns, he stole a .22 rifle and ammunition from a Rhyl fairground. As the police investigated the break-in at the fair, Bassett was heading eastwards towards Delamere Forest, a place he had a fondness for, determined now to end what he would later refer to as 'the uselessness' of his life.

At 10.30 that evening, the French campers pitched their brightly coloured tent in a small clearing by Woodside Lane, Mouldsworth. A number of villagers saw the tent and heard the girls giggling before they settled down for the night.

At 2 am next day, Mr and Mrs Hignett, who lived adjacent to the clearing and who had seen the campers pitch the tent, were awakened by hollow metallic noises, and the sound of a car racing away. They dismissed the disturbance and went back to sleep, but the daylight revealed the horror wrought by those strange sounds.

Monique Liebert.

Roy Walker and Harvey Vickers were making their way to work at a local plant-hire firm, as they did at 7 am every day, when they passed the tent. At first they paid scant attention, but suddenly what they had seen registered with them: a young girl was lying naked and bleeding by the tent. Rushing over to her aid, the two men found she was dead. The girl was Claudine Liebert, and inside the tent, her fiancé Daniel Berland was also dead, while her sister Monique lay dying.

All three had been shot, some 20 bullets pumped into their sleeping bodies. Despite an emergency operation at Chester's Deva Hospital, Monique died later that day, as a murder investigation swung into action at Mouldsworth.

Detective Chief Superintendent Benfield, head of Cheshire CID, who had led the hunt for the 'Moors murderers' in 1965, took charge of the investigation. A link was established between the stolen rifle at Rhyl and the shootings at Mouldsworth when the post-mortem revealed that the bullets used were of the same .22 calibre.

This cold-blooded and seemingly motiveless murder stunned the villagers of Mouldsworth, their grief for the victims coupled with fears for their own safety, for as two days passed the killer remained on the loose. Then late on Tuesday night, 13th July, the manhunt suddenly ceased when a man was found dead in his car near Stone, Staffordshire.

Detective Chief Superintendent Benfield rushed to Stone and the identity of the man who had gunned down the innocent campers was revealed. Michael Bassett had committed suicide in his Ford Escort, choking himself with the fumes from the exhaust. The last words penned by the aspiring writer formed a suicide note, in which he confessed to the murders. It read:

I, Michael Bassett, hereby confess to the murder of these three people. I didn't know what to do about what I had done. I couldn't help myself. They provoked me. I taught them a lesson. I feel the only way to get away from all my lies, sins, failures and general uselessness is to turn myself off.

Cradled under his arm was the stolen rifle with the words: 'It killed three campers' etched into the butt. A torn-up note had also been found by detectives close to Delamere Forest which read: 'The shooter I stole from Rhyl is a good one. It shoots straight. By the time you find this I shall be in a happier place.'

Had Michael Bassett confined himself to terminating only his own

Daniel Berland.

life, then some pity could have been afforded him, but the terrible act of dragging three innocent campers to their deaths led to universal hatred and condemnation.

Their parents wept at the victims' inquest, as Leonard Meadows, the Cheshire Deputy Coroner, and Dr Reuben Woodcock, Home Office pathologist, offered them the sympathies of the whole country. Details of the last moments of what should have been a happy holiday, and of how the three met their deaths, were read aloud.

As the inquest closed, Monsieur André Liebert was given a final poignant reminder of the last days of his two daughters, recalled by Monique in her little red diary.

The parents took their children home for burial in France, the police investigation withdrew, and silence descended once again on the tiny village. With grim irony, a nightingale returned to Mouldsworth soon afterwards. Once so popular, this time there was no rejoicing at its arrival: the villagers' thoughts for the present stayed with those who would never hear birds singing again.

19
THE
DEADLY BARGAIN

The Murder of Albert Buckley at Northwich
March 1986

Fondness for drink can lead to an early grave. The opposite might well be said to be true in the case of the contract killing of a Salvation Army trombonist in the spring of 1986, where it could be argued that by signing the pledge, the victim had signed his own death warrant.

Haulage contractor Albert Buckley first met Christine, his second wife-to-be, at Wrexham sometime during 1980. His first marriage had ended in 1973, and while Christine was at the time living with her husband and two teenage daughters, her own relationship had long been breaking down, and she soon fell for the charms of Buckley despite, or indeed perhaps as it later turned out because of, his hard-drinking, playboy lifestyle. They set up home together in his cottage at Bryneglwys, North Wales, and when her divorce came through in the following year he proposed. On 22nd December 1981, they were married.

A year later the couple moved to Northwich where the new Mrs Buckley became proprietress of the Lunch Box, a café cum sandwich bar on Greenbank Lane, Greenbank, Northwich. They lived in a flat over the café for two years until the death of Buckley's father, which was to be the turning point in their relationship.

Buckley's drinking and womanising ways had been very much against his strict Salvationist family background. Rebelling against the staunch religious practices, Buckley drank heavily until his father's death, when he took a vow of abstinence, signed the pledge and joined the Wrexham Citadel Salvation Army Band as a trombonist.

He also inherited two cottages at Winnington, Northwich, and it was

Albert Buckley.

to one of these, Rose Cottage on Beswicks Road, that he later moved when cracks began to appear in his four year old marriage. Relations between husband and wife had become strained when Buckley began to abstain from their frequent visits to the many pubs where they socialised. Not only did he stop going out drinking, but Buckley now began to preach about the evils of drink and other temptations, to the extent that his wife became exasperated by his pious rantings.

These feelings were compounded when Christine's two teenage daughters, Jane and Patricia, moved in with them. Buckley seemed to take a dislike to the girls, thinking them rude and untidy. He also demanded that Jane, who was now working, should pay for her own upkeep. Mrs Buckley, who considered the family to have a comfortable

Rose Cottage, Beswicks Road, Winnington.

income, refused to accept any money from the teenage girl, and this led to words between Buckley and his wife.

It was during a rare visit together to a public house that Mrs Buckley, more than likely the worse for drink, began to row with her husband. To no one in particular she called out during the quarrel: 'Can someone get rid of my husband? With paraquat!' It was probably said more in jest than with any sincerity but to the man who overheard it, it struck a chord.

Sitting close to the quarrelling Buckleys was 37 year old David Ashbrook, a used-car dealer from Hartford, Northwich. Ashbrook was a reformed crook, who harboured secret ambitions to emulate his hero Charles Bronson in the film *The Mechanic*, in which Bronson plays a hired assassin.

Overhearing Mrs Buckley's outburst, Ashbrook saw the ideal chance to live out his fantasy role. A few days later he approached her, saying he was a member of a Manchester-based organisation that could 'get rid of people for a price'. They arranged to meet up at his home while his wife, a primary school headmistress, was at work, and struck up a deal.

Mrs Buckley agreed to pay Ashbrook a total of £3,500, and also sell him her husband's haulage business, valued at £80,000, for the knock-down price of £20,000. The cash needed for Ashbrook was to be paid in two instalments: the first £1,000 was taken from the café, the remainder would be raised by a bank loan.

A few days later Ashbrook and Mrs Buckley travelled to the Buckleys' cottage in North Wales where, it was later alleged, they began a sexual relationship and from where Ashbrook stole Albert Buckley's shotgun. He sawed down the twin barrels and made preparations to carry out his side of the 'deadly bargain'.

The budding assassin soon found that carrying out his task wasn't as easy as Bronson made it seem in the movies. Three times he made abortive efforts to kill his quarry. Twice Buckley failed to turn up at an ambush Ashbrook had set up. He then borrowed Christine Buckley's car and parked it with the bonnet up on the bypass which Buckley would use on his way home from a Salvation Army meeting in Wrexham, hoping he would think his wife was in distress and stop. Buckley sailed past the attempted ambush, oblivious of his wife's car.

Finally, with the aid of Mrs Buckley, Ashbrook got it right. On Tuesday evening, 25th March 1986, Christine Buckley cooked her husband his tea before he travelled over to Wrexham for band practice.

David Ashbrook being led into court.

She told him she planned to go out drinking at the Red Lion. Sharing a drink with her that night was her husband's next-door neighbour from Beswicks Road, who had been lured away so as not to disturb Ashbrook.

Using a duplicate key, Ashbrook, dressed in combat jacket and balaclava hat, let himself into the cottage and lay in wait. When

114

Christine Buckley being led into court.

Buckley's car headlights signalled his arrival home, Ashbrook squatted on one knee and waited until the kitchen door opened, whereupon he discharged both barrels from a distance of 6 feet. Buckley was killed instantly.

After dumping the gun and changing his clothes, Ashbrook then joined Christine at the Red Lion, intending to give himself an alibi. At 2.30 am, the neighbour returning home came across the dead body of Albert Buckley which was slumped in the doorway. Chief Inspector Frank Morgan took charge of the investigation and immediately questioned the neighbour. He told police he had spent the previous evening drinking with Christine Buckley and that they were later joined at the table by Ashbrook.

Ashbrook was interviewed shortly after dawn. He had already made plans to be out of the country during the murder investigation and had tickets for himself, his wife and young son to spend a week in Tenerife. Detectives questioned Ashbrook about his movements on the previous evening and asked to see his car. Inside the boot of the Mini he had been driving, Ashbrook had left a vital clue linking him with the murder: the gun case and a number of rounds of shot of the same type as that used to kill Mr Buckley.

He was taken to Northwich police station where, after initial denials, he confessed. 'I deeply regret that I have taken this man's life and it distresses me greatly. I don't understand why I did this dreadful deed. I will never forget Albert Buckley.' When told by detectives that her lover had confessed, Christine Buckley also made a full confession, admitting her role in the murder.

Both David Ashbrook and Christine Buckley were charged with murder and exactly one year to the day after the murder, they appeared before Mr Justice French at Chester Crown Court. Mr John Rogers QC outlined the facts of the Crown's case and told the jury it was a carefully planned, clinically carried out killing.

Realising the futility of offering any suggestion that his clients were not guilty, Mr William Waldron QC told the jury that both accused showed great remorse for the murder.

It was a short trial and it ended with the only possible verdict. Addressing the ashen-faced prisoners in the dock, Mr Justice French said that it was a brutal and carefully planned murder. 'The plan was carried out in a remarkably cold-blooded way, both before and after the killing. Nothing has been said which begins to explain why you did what you did.' He then sentenced both the accused to life imprisonment for their parts in the deadly bargain that didn't come off.

20

TAUNTED
OR TEMPTED?

The Murders of Greeba Healey and Marie Walker
at Stockport
July 1986

At sunset, when the last of the day-
trippers have packed up and left for home, the beach at Prestatyn,
North Wales, is a solitary place. On a late July evening in 1986, a
holidaymaker spotted a bundle by the water's edge. Thinking it might
be something of value, he walked over to take a look and saw that it
was a pile of men's clothing which, although soaking wet, was not
discarded tat, but neatly folded and in good condition.

Doubting that the owner could have left his clothes to take a
moonlight swim, the curious finder checked the pockets and
discovered a wallet containing a handwritten note. The wallet belonged
to 37 year old Robert Healey, of Longmead Avenue, Stockport, and the
note was addressed to his mother. It read: 'My marriage is over, there's
nothing left to live for – I might as well die now.'

The man called the police, who began to investigate the apparent
suicide of Mr Healey. Detectives at Stockport called at the house on
Longmead Avenue and finding no one at home, made a thorough
search of the property. Missing from the house, besides Healey, were
his 40 year old wife Greeba and 13 year old stepdaughter, Marie
Walker.

Another 'suicide note' was found at the house. This was addressed to
Healey's wife. It began: 'Dear Greeba, it seems I am unable to love you
the way you want . . .' and ended: 'I hope the crabs eat my body.'

Suspicions that police might be dealing with foul play were aroused
when bloodstains were spotted in the Healeys' bedroom, and these
were compounded when a number of videotapes were found on a

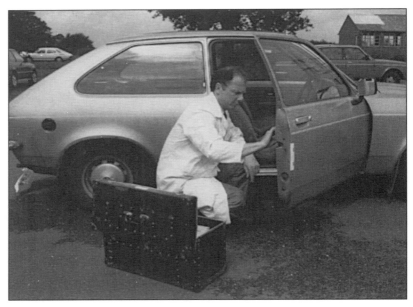

The Healeys' family car being examined by forensic experts at the Science Laboratory in Chorley, Lancs.

shelf. The tapes that caught the eye were episodes of the television series *The Fall and Rise of Reginald Perrin*, in which the central character fakes his own suicide by leaving his clothes on a beach, and starts a new life elsewhere.

By 5th August, it was established that a silver Vauxhall Chevette left in a Birmingham car park since the previous Thursday, the day after the suggested suicide, belonged to Robert Healey, who had last been seen driving away from his Stockport home two days earlier.

There were now grave fears for the safety of Greeba Healey and Marie Walker, and having discounted the suicide as a fake, Detective Chief Superintendent Clive Atkinson announced in the press: 'I am making a personal appeal to Robert Healey to come forward and speak to me, or any police officer, to relieve the anguish of his wife's parents, his wife's friends and his stepdaughter's father.'

On the following day, Wednesday 6th August, the bloodstains from Longmead Avenue were found to prove a forensic match for the blood group of the mother and daughter who had been missing since

118

Longmead Avenue, Stockport.

lunchtime on the previous Monday, and later that evening Chief Superintendent Atkinson announced that he was now treating the case as a murder hunt and was very anxious to trace Mr Healey.

Gossip about the family's disappearance was rife. Robert Healey, a self-employed taxi driver, had met Greeba through a lonely hearts advertisement in the local paper. Curtains had often twitched on Longmead Avenue in the past when Greeba had stood in the garden of their home shouting at her husband: 'You don't want me, you don't love me!'

The speculation continued when on Saturday 9th August, a quilt discovered in a ditch near the A5117, close to Chester, was found to contain bloodstains which again matched those of Greeba and Marie. The silver Vauxhall found in the Birmingham car park also contained matching bloodstains.

An RAF helicopter with heat-seeking equipment was used to help search for the bodies near where the duvet was found, and as the days passed, hopes of finding the missing women faded.

On Friday evening, 15th August, 72 year old William Douglas unwittingly achieved what sophisticated equipment had thus far failed to do. Walking in woods at Caerwys, North Wales, he kicked a pile of leaves and discovered the shallow graves of Greeba and Marie.

News of the discovery of the decomposing bodies appeared in the national press. Realising arrest was now only a matter of time, Robert Healey, who had been living under the assumed name of Maurice Beach, at an address in Kensal Green, west London, gave himself up at New Scotland Yard on the following evening. He was returned to Stockport and charged with murdering Greeba Healey and Marie Walker on 29th July 1986. He denied the charges and was remanded in custody pending trial.

At Liverpool Crown Court on Monday 23rd March 1987, the jury heard evidence from Home Office pathologist Dr Donald Wayte that Greeba Healey had died of multiple skull fractures, whilst Marie had been suffocated. He added that the nature of Marie's suffocation was consistent with that of victims crushed to death in road accidents.

Healey himself was called to the witness box by his defence counsel, Mr John Hugell QC. He told the court that he had met Greeba through a lonely hearts column in 1985. He said that things were all right between them until after the marriage, when she started to become obsessive towards him, and wanted him to be constantly with her.

Robert and Greeba Healey.

Asked about the events of 29th July, Healey said it was like watching a film:

'The trouble started when Greeba criticised my love-making. I felt like screaming, I was so frustrated. I walked down to the kitchen and saw the rolling pin. I went back upstairs to our bedroom and hit her on the head with it. She jumped up, but didn't say anything: she didn't scream, she just moaned. I hit her again, I don't know how many times. Eventually she was down on the floor. Marie came in and I told her to get out. She did so but came straight back in again. I didn't want her to see her mother on the floor. I grabbed her by the throat and pushed her against the wall. The next thing I remember, she was down on the floor. I don't know how long it was before I realised they were both dead. I didn't know what I was doing.'

Mr Brian Leveson QC, prosecuting, intended to prove, however, that Robert Healey was perfectly lucid during the attack and that there was a more sinister reason than frustration and marital strife for the double murder.

Dispelling the notion of a man out of his mind, he explained to the

Police frogmen search for the bodies of the missing women.

jury how, after bludgeoning his wife, Healey took steps to remove evidence by cleaning the rolling pin, washing down walls spattered with blood, and changing the bedlinen, which was now also stained with Greeba's blood.

He put the bodies into his wife's car and left a note, cancelling the milk and newspapers. He also applied for a passport in his brother-in-law's name, before placing his clothes on Prestatyn beach in an attempt to fake suicide. Referring to this, Mr Leveson asked Healey:

'Doesn't Reginald Perrin, the TV character, do what you did?'

'Yes,' Healey replied, 'but I didn't get the ideas from a programme. I fully intended to commit suicide.'

Prosecution counsel then referred to the pathologist's report, which showed that both Greeba and her daughter had sexual intercourse just before their deaths. He asked Healey: 'Were you engaging in sexual intercourse with your stepdaughter Marie? Was it not the case that she had threatened to expose you for this, so you killed her?'

'Nothing of the sort!' Healey replied.

On the seventh day of the trial, after summing up the key points, Mr Justice McNeill addressed the jury before they were asked to consider a verdict. There was no dispute over whether Healey had actually killed his wife and stepdaughter, but the jury were asked to consider whether Mrs Healey or Marie had caused provocation. Referring to the assault on Mrs Healey, the judge asked: 'Would a reasonable man take a rolling pin and rain blows down on her head so as to kill her?'

Apparently not, thought the jury and after three hours' consideration they returned a unanimous guilty verdict. Mr Justice McNeill then sentenced Healey to two terms of life imprisonment.

What was not revealed at the trial, however, was that Healey had previously been put on two years' probation, in 1983, for inciting a young girl to an act of gross indecency.

As no motive for the murders was established, opinion remains divided: did Robert Healey murder because he was taunted by his wife; or was he afraid of exposure, as a man unable to resist the temptation to assault his stepdaughter? Greeba and Marie can never tell; only Robert Healey really knows the truth.

ACKNOWLEDGEMENTS

A number of people helped during the research and writing of *Cheshire Murder Casebook*, and in this respect I am particularly grateful to Wilf Gregg, David Mossop and Matthew Spicer who helped to locate information on a number of cases, and also to Lisa Moore for her help and support.

My thanks must also go to the staffs at libraries in Bolton, Birkenhead, Ellesmere Port, Manchester and Northwich, who all went to great lengths to supply research material.

For help with photographs and other illustrations, I would like to thank Adrian Greenhalgh at the Bolton Institute; Alison Surtees; Kath and Paul at the *Manchester Evening News*; the staff at Chester Archives; and PLT pictures.

We have tried to trace the copyright owners of all the pictures used, but apologise if we have inadvertently contravened any existing copyright.

Finally, I would like to thank Nicholas and Suzanne Battle and the staff at Countryside Books for helping me put together my third book in the Murder Casebook series.

INDEX

125